What Reader

"*Church Ecology* is a practical tool that assists church leaders and faith communities in developing a discipleship pathway that fosters a greater capacity for leadership development and transformational ministry. Kelly and Ken provide a biblical and theological framework that invites the readers to think afresh of how one understands the church as an ecosystem and its ability to rethink, recreate and reset for greater vitality and witness. The prayers and reflection questions provide an opportunity for the reader to intentionally engage this leadership pathway process."

Bishop Tracy S. Malone
Resident Bishop, East Ohio Conference of the United Methodist Church

"Willard and Brown bring their vast experience, skills, gifts, and wisdom together to create this much-needed resource on intentional leadership development. They brilliantly illustrate how leadership is a key component of a church's ecosystem. The authors reveal how the health, vitality, fruitfulness, and effectiveness of the church's ability to live out its mission rises and falls in relationship to its leadership. This is a must-read for all those who are leaders, who will be leaders, and who are raising up new leaders."

Kay Kotan,
Director, Center for Multiplying Disciples, Arkansas Conference UMC

"The authors recognize The Church as the Body of Christ, with a clear orderly functioning life. Attention to the living cells within, especially the leadership, helps to make for a healthy Church. This book clearly helps to focus the reader on the healthy, deliberate life of The Body of Christ as lived directly in local congregations."

W. Michie Klusmeyer
Bishop, Episcopal Diocese of West Virginia

"Leadership theories and ideas are important, equally important is how to put these into action. This would be a great book for clergy to read with their leadership team. Prayers, exercises and practical ideas can move a church into developing a pathway for leaders for years to come."

Rev. Julie Hager Love
President/CEO, Kentucky United Methodist Children's Homes

"Brown and Willard have come together to offer the church a most thoughtful and accessible read on Leader Development. This book, anchored in Scripture and prayer, efficiently equips and engages us to take seriously the spiritual gift of leadership. I have not seen a growing and transformed church that does not have a gifted, thoughtful and prayerful leadership across its life, and I believe that this book can contribute to the overall healthy and poised for growth ecosystem of the Body of Christ."

The Reverend Thaddaeus B. Allen
Regional Minister and President the Christian Church
(Disciples of Christ) in West Virginia

"As Willard made strides by asking churches to examine how they sought to make disciples, Brown and Willard provide an ecologically-friendly pathway for finding and developing leaders that moves beyond a frantic search in the fall of the year to an ongoing process for identifying and equipping leaders who are invited to live into their giftedness. The Leadership Covenant provided in the appendix reinforces what churches expect from growing leaders who grow leaders."

Phil Schroeder
Director of the Center for Congregational Excellence
North Georgia Conference of the United Methodist Church

"Churches can no longer afford to ignore their leadership development pathways. *Church Ecology: Creating a Leadership Pathway for Your Church* not only challenges us to think about how we already do this but provides lots of practical ideas on how we can strengthen our ministry by being more intentional about this important aspect of church life."

Ed Thompson
General Presbyter, Prebytery of West Virginia

"*Church Ecology* is a stand-out work in a plethora of books about church leadership. With just enough theory to provide background, this resource is full of practical advice and methodology for creating a leader development process in any size congregation. In a church culture longing for stronger leadership, this book is a gem! Kudos to Ken and Kelly for recognizing the direct link between maturing disciples and the development of effective leaders."

Phil Maynard
Author of Shift 2.0: Helping Congregations Back Into the Game of Effective Ministry

"*Church Ecology* is more than just another resource on church leadership. Reading these pages will inspire you to create an environment in your local church that is healthy, thriving and unique to your context. Examining the varied challenges and complexity of leadership, this read sets up the potential for true congregational transformation"

Ken Nash
Lead Pastor, Watermark Wesleyan Church

Church
Ecology

Creating a
Leadership
Pathway
for Your
Church

Ken Willard & Kelly Brown

Introduction by Bishop Sandra Steiner Ball

Market
Square
BOOKS

Church Ecology

Creating a Leadership Pathway for Your Church

books@marketsquarebooks.com
P.O. Box 23664 Knoxville, Tennessee 37933

ISBN: 978-1-950899-10-4
Library of Congress: 2019956135

Printed and Bound in the United States of America
Cover Illustration & Book Design ©2019 Market Square Publishing, LLC

Publisher: Kevin Slimp
Editor: Kristin Lighter
Post-Process Editor: Ken Rochelle

**Unless otherwise noted, Scripture quotations
from the Common English Bible:**

Table of Contents

Acknowledgements

This book would not be possible without Morning Star Church and especially pastor Mike Schreiner. Little did I know back in 1999, when my family and I attended the very first service for Morning Star Church, how much the next almost twenty years with MSC and Mike's leadership would influence my ministry. Mike Schreiner is clearly a contributor to this book, but he is also much more than that. He is my friend and the reason I was able to find my true calling in life when my world had been shaken to its core. Many of the leadership concepts and lessons in this book come from our work together developing pastors and laity leaders in our church and beyond.

Before moving full time into the church world, I spent many years learning and teaching leadership with Lechmere, Target, Linens 'N Things, and OfficeMax, along with doing some contract work with Daikin and the Transportation Security Administration. Those organizations and the leaders I have worked with have had an influence on my personal leadership style development, the ministry I have done, and the ministry work I continue to do today.

I would also like to acknowledge the many churches and pastors I've coached over the years, and the many ministry leaders at all levels who have challenged and encouraged me along the way, allowing me to speak a little into their own leadership development. A special acknowledgement to Dr. J. Val Hastings, the president and founder of Coaching-4Clergy, for his leadership and guidance over the years.

There are two people, along with Mike Schreiner, who have had the most influence in my journey and deserve special acknowledgement—Dr. David Hyatt and Kay Kotan. You have been my partners, and will always be my friends. Thanks for walking with me as we equip leaders in God's Kingdom.

Most of all, my wife Mary and our daughter Amanda who is waiting for us in heaven.

Ken Willard

I want to express my love, gratitude, and appreciation to generations of family that have shaped me into the person I am today. Firstly, my grandparents, Cochran and Shibler, who modeled love and grace to me. Secondly, many aunts, uncles, and cousins who helped me experience countless adventures in my life and impacted how I see the world every day. My parents, Ken and Doris, whose unending love and witness of faith started me on my own journey of faith, leading to a calling in vocational ministry. My brothers and sister Ken, Susan, and Keith, exhibited patience and guidance, allowing me to be the energetic little brother. Finally, and most importantly, my wife Amy, son Jacob, and daughter Josie (who helped me with research for this book). Their encouragement inspires me to be a better person everyday; I cannot do anything without their support and love. These family relationships have and continue to bless me in countless ways.

Kelly P. Brown

Introduction

When I think of church as an ecosystem, it takes me back to an illustration and quote that I used in my Doctor of Ministry work and thesis: "You are more than what you have become." This quote from the 1994 Disney animated film, *The Lion King,* comes at a point in the action where the circle of life—the ecosystem of the Pride Rock community (which is home to the lion family and a host of other animal species)—has become unbalanced and therefore unhealthy. Leadership has been interrupted, usurped by Scar, and the true heir, Simba, has been chased off, scared away. Scar has served to unbalance and destabilize the community – it's inhabitants and the environment – literally scarring it, wounding it deeply, almost to the point of death. Leadership has damaged the health of the ecosystem.

The members of the community are not working and serving together. Attention to the health of the environment and the interconnectedness of the members of the community has gone by the wayside. Relationships have been broken. Boundaries set up for the safety and protection of the community have been crossed. Resources have been eaten up and depleted without any thought or plan for replacing, renewing, or growing toward a future. The hope for generative living and life is almost nonexistent. The whole ecosystem – the entire community – seems to be on the edge of collapse when the true heir is discovered alive, invited to return, challenged to remember who he is, and confronted with the fact that he is more than what he has become.

Just like in nature, the health of a church ecosystem can be interrupted and influenced by a change in the balance of resources, interactions, and relationships. Therefore leadership, and building intentional pathways for discovering and developing leaders, is vitally important. Indeed, the key to keeping the ecology of a community healthy is leadership. The health and fruitfulness of a church ecosystem depends on the ability to discover, invite, develop, engage, and generate leaders who understand that they and the communities they serve have been created by God to be more than they have become.

Clergy and lay leadership in the church changes from time to time for a variety of reasons – it can be expected and known ahead of time, or like in *The Lion King,* it can be sudden, dramatic, or tragic. Is your congregation prepared? Has your family of faith planned for and created a leadership pathway for your church? If not, *Church Ecology: Creating a Leadership Pathway for Your Church* is a resource that will spiritually ground you in a process to create a leadership pathway that fits your church and its context of ministry and mission. Creating an effective leadership pathway helps congregations to intentionally raise up leaders who can work with others in the local church system to evaluate the balance of interrelationships among people and the community context, and who influence the church ecosystem towards generative health and growth in mission and ministry.

Church Ecology invites all of us to remember that God has in fact created us to be more than we have become. Called by Christ to discipleship, we are the true heirs of Christ. We are called to share the gifts that God has given to each of us on behalf of the whole community so that we can more effectively be the body of Christ in and for the world today. As a part of that call, we have a responsibility to discover, and sometimes re-discover, those whom God has gifted for leadership and invite them to prayerfully consider God's direction or call for their lives. A leadership pathway helps us to intentionally discover potential leaders and to help them develop their skills and multiply their experience. It allows for coaching, growth, and spiritual formation by helping potential leaders to remember who they are in Christ. They have been named and claimed in their baptism not only to belong to a community of leaders, but to become a leader like Jesus, and to bless others through their leadership. Leadership pathways also help the larger church community to support and nurture these persons as they allow God's Spirit to transform them into the greater design God has for their lives and for the healthy growth of our church communities.

Ken and Kelly lay out a practical step-by-step approach to creating a leadership pathway that is grounded in scripture and prayer. Their creative, reflective process and practical suggestions invite all who participate to remember who they are in Christ. They take the theoretical and give a variety of practical applications emphasizing that each church must develop its own leadership pathway according to its cultural, missional, and ministry context. The approach they suggest to developing a leadership pathway invites curiosity. They invite us to be curious about current leadership development processes, curious about what those processes could be, curious about the journey – past, present, and future – and curious about past, present, and future capacity for fruitfulness. They invite us to ask questions and they ask us questions, coaching us to determine the next appropriate action step for our unique church situation. They also remind us that a leadership pathway for a community should not be built or created by one person, but a diverse small group of persons who are passionate about growing a healthy and generative church ministry, outreach, and witness.

We are more than we have become. *Church Ecology* helps us to focus on and facilitate the more God has created us to be. It invites us to anticipate and prepare for future leadership in the church. Instead of leaving the development of church leadership up to happenstance, which opens the door to persons that could potentially *"Scar"* the fruitfulness and life of a church ecosystem for a long time into the future, Ken and Kelly invite us to anticipate and to prepare for future leadership through an intentional process of creating a leadership pathway that empowers us to live a healthy, balanced life with Christ and one another as the church. Developing a leadership pathway serves to open up endless possibilities for us to be one with Christ, one with each other, and one in God's transforming ministry to all the world – not just for the moment, but for the future. Indeed, empowering us to become "the more" that God designed and created us to be both as Christ's disciples and the church.

Bishop Sandra Steiner Ball

West Virginia Annual Conference of The United Methodist Church

CHAPTER ONE

The Church as an Ecosystem

"Clearly, the Lord owns the sky, the highest heavens, the earth, and everything in it."

Deuteronomy 10:14

"Never doubt that a small group of thoughtful, committed citizens can change the world; indeed, it is the only thing that ever has."

Margaret Mead

Fifty years ago, when a spark from a passing train ignited the oil-slicked floating debris on the Cuyahoga River in Cleveland, Ohio, people realized that a dying, polluted river was also killing the community. In twenty to thirty minutes, the fire reached over five stories. For years, the Cuyahoga River was one of the most polluted rivers in the country; this was not the first time it had caught on fire. The river's unhealthiness and death caused the death and unhealthiness of the vegetation, bugs, fish, and birds which would normally populate the watershed. The polluted river was also killing Lake Erie, which it flowed into. The river fire of 1969 led to Cleveland being nicknamed the "mistake by the lake" and, more importantly, this accelerated a national movement focused on clean air and water. In 1970, the Environmental Protection Agency was established to manage environmental risks and regulate policy relating to clean air and water.

...nothing exists as an end to itself.

In the years since the Cuyahoga River fire, many steps have been taken to clean up all the environments that the river affects. These changes have been successful. More bugs and vegetation flourish along the river shores. The growth in bugs and vegetation has in turn increased the bird and bee population. The river is also now filled with a diverse fish population which, among other things, has brought the bald eagle back to the region. Based on these facts, it is clear that when the Cuyahoga River is healthy, the health of everything it touches increases. This real-life example illustrates the concept that nothing exists as an end to itself.

We are connected to other humans and the created world. This understanding of existence also means that the health of one element of our world impacts the health of the whole system. In our personal lives, if we are surrounded by people who have toxic relationships, our personal health and relationships will be affected. The same is true in nature. The well-being of one part of creation affects the health of the whole system.

The scientific term for this interconnectedness of everything is *ecosystem*. An ecosystem is a community of living and nonliving components and their various types of relationships interacting as a system for life. In many ways, a church can fit the same definition of an ecosystem. It is an interconnected community of people working and serving together as a system for life. This community interacts with the uniqueness, the demographics, and economic factors existing in the mission field of the environment around them. Additionally, by describing the church as an ecosystem, it is established that the church is a living organism that needs tended to and developed. As Bill Easum expressed in his book *Leadership on The Other Side* the church is not a machine where the solution to ineffectiveness is replacement of broken parts. Instead, the church is organic and needs consistent and capable care to ensure vital fruitful ministry. Each component of the ecosystem must be nurtured in an effective way to ensure its purpose is being fulfilled for the whole community. Similar to nature's ecosystem, the health of a church's ecosystem is influenced by many things—even the smallest variation within it can bring about dynamic change in the overall system. This can lead to a healthier ecosystem or an unhealthier ecosystem. The biggest influencer of a healthy church ecosystem is leadership. Healthy leaders lead healthy churches, and healthy churches grow.

> Healthy leaders lead healthy churches, and healthy churches grow.

Ecologists find it difficult to label an ecosystem as healthy, just as it is difficult to define congregational health. In nature, each environment is so diverse that health is defined differently for each. The staple components of an ecosystem are soil, water, and atmosphere. Keeping those three things healthy and in balance is the key to a vital ecosystem. The balance of these is not measured by hard and fast rules but, instead, by markers that indicate health for the specific setting and environment. The question for the church is, "What are the key markers which indicate their ecosystem is healthy?" We often use metrics of attendance for this evaluation, but these markers go deeper than how many people attend worship or small groups. The real indicator is that the church is moving toward its desired outcome and is making a defined difference in the community, because the healthier the church is, the healthier the community is around it.

- Many churches and church leaders struggle with any type of ministry numbers. Similar to ecologists, leaders in the church count so that we can measure. Consider a couple who takes their newborn child to the doctor. On the first visit, the child will be weighed and measured to determine its height and weight. On every subsequent visit, the child will be weighed and measured again. This is done to see if the child is growing. Does a growing child provide proof that the child is healthy? No. Does a non-growing child always indicate that the child is unhealthy? No. But these measurements help the doctor to know when they need to pay more attention, ask more questions, go a little deeper to determine health or an issue. The same is true with statistics such as average worship attendance. Is a church with more people in worship this year versus last year guaranteed to be healthy? No. Neither is a church with less people in worship this year versus last year guaranteed to be unhealthy. Those are just indicators of health that should lead church leaders to go deeper and ask more questions.

In his book *Doing the Math of Mission: Fruits, Faithfulness, and Metrics* author Gil Rendle offers the following definitions:

- *Counting* is giving attention to numbers. When counting, the question to be answered is "How many?" Conversations about "How many?" are most frequently conversations about resources.

- *Measuring* is giving attention to change. When measuring, the question is not "How many?" but rather "How far?" Conversations about "How far?" are frequently about change that can be measured over time, as in "How far have we come, over the past year, toward our goal?

So, we count things such as average attendance in worship, professions of faith, adults baptized this year, children baptized this year, professing members, adults in Christian formation, vacation Bible school attendance, first-time guests, etc. *so that* we are able to measure how we are doing toward our mission.

The key to keeping the ecology of the church vibrant is leadership. We can compare this to the role of the ecologist in nature. An ecologist studies the interrelationship between creatures and their environment. In this way, a church leader is measuring how the culture of the church and the people within it are interacting to create a healthy, vital system focused on a mission to change the world. The ecologist is constantly evaluating the ecosystem to determine if things are in balance and if it is moving toward the markers of health, which point toward the difference the church is called to make.

At the end of each chapter, we will provide a set of questions. These questions are based on the topics of the chapter and designed to help you take what you have just read to see ways to apply the information to your specific ministry.

Imagine Kelly and Ken sitting with you as you read each chapter and then asking you a few coaching questions. We encourage you not to skip over these questions or to just read them and then move on. Pause for a few minutes. Capture your responses on paper or some electronic form so you can refer back to them as you move through the book. While we both have a lot of experience working with all types of churches, pastors, and laity leaders all over the country, chances are great that we are not as familiar with you and your ministry as you are. These questions provide you an opportunity to take large concepts, examples different from your context, and general items and make them specific to you and your church. This is a very critical process in order to move from merely *information* to *application*.

We will also end each chapter with a prayer. This is our way of praying for you and your ministry on this journey to create a leadership development process in your church. Hear us speaking these words over you. Know we pray for God's Spirit to guide you and support you with all you need, and more than you can ever hope for or imagine.

Before you move to the next chapter, take a few minutes now to answer the following questions:

What surprises you about seeing the church as an ecosystem?

How healthy is your ministry now? What signs have you seen that indicate you need to tend to the health of your church in a new way?

Where is it time to do some pruning in your ministry in order to see more fruit for God's Kingdom?

Prayer

Lord, we are always amazed at the beauty in the world you created all around us: deserts, oceans, green fields, mountains, valleys, lakes, and so much more. We pray that we might be good stewards of this world you have provided us and leave it better than it was when we arrived. We pray the same for our churches. Help us to honor you as leaders and as a part of your wonderful creation. Amen.

CHAPTER TWO

Prayer, Scripture, and Preparation

And I tell you: Ask and you will receive. Seek and you will find. Knock and the door will be opened to you. Everyone who asks, receives. Whoever seeks, finds. To everyone who knocks, the door is opened.

Luke 11:9-10

I start with the premise that the function of leadership is to produce more leaders, not more followers.

Ralph Nader

Great things begin with prayer. As you go on this journey of creating a leadership pathway for your ministry it is important to set the right foundation. This might start with you, but we would encourage you to expand the circle beyond just yourself. Pray for wisdom and discernment, pray for the Holy Spirit to guide your journey, pray for the leaders in your church now and those who God will be bringing to you in the future. Does your church have a prayer ministry now? Ask them to add this process of leadership development to their prayer list. Be sure to bring your staff, other ministry leaders, and all of the current leaders in your church into this prayer initiative.

What would you do if one day God called you to be a missionary overseas? You clearly feel God sending you to a location you have never been to, and a culture you know nothing about. Most likely you would start learning about that culture and location. You would hopefully start with prayer, do a lot of research, *pray*, talk to people who have been there, *pray*, and prepare yourself. There are a lot of similarities between this leadership journey and becoming an overseas missionary. We strongly encourage you to cover the process in prayer. We believe God has given each ministry the resources needed to carry out the work God is calling them to do. This includes leaders. Pray for God to lead this process. Pray for the Holy Spirit to guide conversations and to provide wisdom and discernment along the way. Over the years, we have heard from many pastors and church leaders who are struggling with finding new leaders for their ministry. Our first question is always, "Have you been praying about this?" How about you? Pause your reading for a minute now and speak to God about your challenges and struggles concerning leadership in your ministry. Then listen to what the Holy Spirit is saying.

There was a new church years ago that was having a lot of challenges finding someone to fill a key position in their music ministry. After exhausting all of their ideas and possibilities with no results, the ministry leader went to the church's leadership team and asked for prayers. The leadership team stopped their meeting and prayed. The next week three people suddenly appeared who were all qualified for that position! Has this ever happened to you? How often is prayer our last resort instead of our first step?

A rapidly growing church was looking for a new pastor to add to their staff. They did a nationwide search and found many qualified and experienced candidates, but no one felt like the right fit for their church. The pastor and staff began to pray for God to give them the discernment they needed to find the right person for their ministry. It turned out that there was a pastor who had been worshiping with them for several weeks who was the perfect fit! God had answered their prayers and they did not even know it. We believe that God has provided each church with the resources (people, money, facilities, etc.) they need to carry out the ministry God is calling them to do.

> God has provided you with all the resources you need to carry out the ministry God is calling you to do.

As you and your church are spending time in prayer for this leadership initiative, we would also encourage you to spend time in God's Word. Search the Scriptures with a lens of leadership development. Where do you see examples of God calling people into leadership positions? Notice how often God is using people who do not see themselves as leaders, and even people who are not seen as leaders by those around them. Two great resources for you and your leaders to use are the Wesley Study Bible and the John Maxwell Leadership Bible. We would also encourage you and your leaders to look through the Gospels for specific areas where Jesus is modeling leadership with his disciples. Go deeper than just what was said. Study how the greatest leader of all time was teaching and modeling leadership for three years to a ragtag group of people—most of whom never saw themselves as leaders—and who went on to start a movement that changed the world.

Leaders tend to be people of action. This is a very good thing! We are not encouraging you to slow down or to create barriers in any way. We are suggesting that you ensure a strong foundation of prayer and study prior to moving too quickly into creating a leadership pathway for your church. This investment of time and prayer will pay off in the long term with a more fruitful process designed to last more than just a season or two.

The following are a few examples of how you might begin this new process of leadership development in your church with prayers. Pick one or two which seem to best fit you and your ministry and put them in place now.

- List out all of the current leaders in your church on 3x5 index cards, one person on each card. Set a time each day to pray for one of your leaders as you hold their card. Thank God for them and their gifts, pray for God's Spirit to guide them and their lives, and pray for this to be a season of leadership growth for both them and their ministry.

- Schedule a Day of Prayer retreat for all of your leaders. If possible, use an off-site facility so you will not have the normal distractions of using a familiar location. Assign each leader a short devotion based on a different leader in the Bible. Make this time of prayer a chance for you and your team to grow as both leaders and disciples. (Consider including people who are not currently serving in a leadership role, maybe up-and-coming leaders, or maybe those who you see the gift of leadership but are not yet serving in a leadership capacity in the ministry.)

• Have your leadership team practice prayer walking together each time they meet. For five to ten minutes each time, send them out in pairs to walk the community around your church and to pray over everything and everyone they see. Encourage them to spend most of the time just listening to what God is saying to them and what God is showing them as they walk. If you can do this immediately prior to your meeting this would allow you to start each session with a quick debrief and collective prayer.

• Create a list of community leaders (police chief, fire chief, school principal, business owners, local government officials, etc.) and pray for one or two by name during each of your meetings. Grow your perspective in what leadership looks like and the many types of leaders God has placed all around your ministry.

• Use the Wesley Study Bible or the Maxwell Leadership Bible in your leadership meetings to focus each time on a different leader in scripture who you can learn from due to either their situation or their unique skills. End each study time with a prayer for God to equip your leaders to best guide your congregation through the challenges of today.

• Make a list of Christian leaders you admire throughout history, such as John Wesley, Dr. Martin Luther King, Jr., Francis Asbury, Mother Theresa, Dietrich Bonhoeffer, etc. Try to include some leaders your church leadership team might not be very familiar with, or at least might not know as much about. Assign each member of your leadership team one leader from history. Ask them to learn enough about the leader as they can, and come back to share both their story and a few lessons for today with everyone.

- Spend time in prayer as you review the listing of first-time guests, new members, or others who may be new to your church. Pray for discernment to recognize new leaders, especially those who may not fit the mold of your current leaders.

> If diversity is not already present in your leadership, it must be sought out and recruited.

A quick word about this journey to create a leadership pathway for your church. Don't try to do this alone. Prayerfully gather at least two or three others to take this journey with you. If you were to try and do this alone, as good as your intentions might be, you would likely create a leadership pathway perfectly designed for YOU! Look for leaders who are as diverse as possible, in all senses of the word. Leaders who have a variety of experiences and who can help you and each other see new possibilities. In nature, when ecosystems are diverse, more oxygen is produced, more photosynthesis takes place, and water is purified. This is a result of biodiversity. Biodiversity must be present in our leaders in order to create a healthy church ecosystem. The diversity that is needed must be in age, gender, ethnicity, culture, and economic background. If the diversity is not already present in your leadership, it must be sought out and recruited. Diversity cannot be the ideal, it must be the standard. These diverse leaders create space for new ideas and provide a fresh perspective—without which, the ecosystem cannot be healthy. We feel it is very important to have the voice of next generation leaders in this group so that your pathway will be able to equip and reach new leaders. If possible, gather your small group of leadership pathway development leaders together now and give them each a copy of this book so they can take the full journey with you.

Building on this foundation of prayer, the next chapter will focus on gaining a clear picture of where your church has been, is now, and will move into in the area of leadership development. The question we hope you can answer is, "In your life as a disciple and a congregation, in the next chapter of your life, what difference is God calling you to make?"

Before you move to the next chapter, take a few minutes now to answer the following questions:

Who are you going to partner with on this journey to create a new leadership pathway for your church?

Which one or two of the prayer suggestions listed above are you going to put into practice?

What has God's Spirit been saying to you as you read this chapter?

Prayer

Lord, we are thankful for all the ways you have gifted us and our ministry. We pray for those in all areas of leadership throughout our church and our community. May your Spirit guide us this season as we strive to grow closer to you and to be good stewards of your gifts. Help us to grow as leaders who grow leaders. Amen.

CHAPTER THREE

Study the System

Get wisdom; get understanding. Don't forget and don't turn away from my words. Don't abandon her, and she will guard you. Love her, and she will protect you. The beginning of wisdom: Get wisdom! Get understanding before anything else.

Proverbs 4:5-7

Every system is perfectly designed to get the results it gets.

Paul Batalden

Have you ever used a GPS system to get you to a new location? In the old days, when someone was going on a trip to a new location, they had to rely on paper maps. Today, we can just type in an address to our phones and get turn-by-turn directions to just about anywhere. What we sometimes forget is that for our smart-phone GPS to give us directions, it needs two things: where we are going and where we are currently. As we begin the process of studying the leadership system, we need to start with where we are now. We add to that information where we have been and what is the difference God is calling us to make in the next chapter of our lives. Those three elements together can be referred to as hindsight, insight, and foresight. (Hindsight is where we have been, insight is where we are now, and foresight is where we are going.)

> Hindsight is where we have been, insight is where we are now, and foresight is where we are going.

In nature, an ecosystem's past affects its future health. The first way this occurs is called *secondary succession*, defined as when an existing environment is disturbed or changed in a negative way such as by fire, flood, or radioactivity. This change creates the necessity for a new start. The new beginning occurs when a few, but strong, plants grow again. As a result of these new starts, the system is attractive to new species of animals and plants and becomes more diverse. In nature, as in the church, this drastic destruction is caused by *human interference*. Human interference is an unexpected, sudden change that is always harmful. In the life of the church, out of this conflict, new diverse leadership must be developed to ensure a strong start to a vital community.

Contrastly, *succession climax* is the final stage of an ecosystem, where it has the smallest risk for interference and harm. What makes a succession climax ecosystem healthy is its *cyclic succession*.

Cyclic succession is a natural process that leads to healthy changes on a cyclical basis. In nature, this may be a plant that has been dormant, but now springs up and brings changes to the ecosystem. In considering where your church has been in leadership development, are you recovering from a drastic destructive conflict where you must develop new, diverse leaders? Or are you building on an ever-present momentum growing leaders to succeed those who are already serving? It is important to remember that both ecosystems have the potential to be healthy, they just need to take different paths.

How has your leadership development been in the past? We understand that it has likely not been what you want, since you are reading this book, but it is still important to gather this information. Another element of this research into your leadership past is to look at who has been serving in leadership positions in your church. Not just their names, but how did they become a leader in your church? What did they do outside your ministry? What leadership gifts did they have and how did they grow and develop those gifts? Look for trends in the types of leaders your church has had in the past along with where they came from. What have been some of the highlights of leadership and leadership development in your church? What have been some of the ongoing challenges you have faced concerning church leadership?

We know some of this information may be challenging to find. Gather what you can and resist getting frustrated or just throwing up your hands and giving up. Each small piece of information you find is a piece of the puzzle and will help you later on in this leadership development process. If you are new to the church, be sure to speak with others who have been there longer and may be able to provide you with additional insights into church leadership history.

A small church in a rural part of the country might

go through this process and discover a time in their past where most of their ministry leaders worked for a local coal company. Over the years, the coal mine was closed and most of the leaders came from the railroad industry. When that industry changed and those leaders left town, the leaders seemed to come from all different types of areas (teachers, bankers, stay-at-home moms, restaurant owners, etc.). The church learned, or was forced to learn, how to diversify where their leaders came from and it actually made them stronger.

Another example of a radical change to a system of healthy development was the history of Acadia National Park. In 1947, there was a wildfire that destroyed 20 percent of the forest. Following the fire, a few initial plants sprung up and recolonized the area. Formerly, the forest was full of evergreens. However, now it has diversified with many different types of plants. With a few strong leaders, a new diverse life can be made that strengthens the whole environment, even from such a paralyzing tragedy.

Your church leadership history will be different, but still important to understand as we move forward. One way to gather some of this insight into church leadership might be to review the overall history of your church. Pay special attention to the origin story of the ministry and to any times of conflict. While church leadership trends might not be named outright, you should be able to gain a good feeling of leadership behaviors and areas of focus.

Once you have a picture of where the church has been in the past for leadership development (hindsight), it is time to move to where you are today (insight). This perspective of where you are now should also include some elements outside your church. For example, we encourage you to utilize a resource such as MissionInsite to obtain information about your community and mission field. Many of us assume we know the communities where we live and where our churches are located. The truth is that we are creatures of habit and what we really know are the paths we take, the places we shop, the restaurants where we eat, the roads we take to and from work; you get the idea. An objective look at the community can give us a whole new insight into where God has called us to lead. The statistical data is of course not the whole picture, but it is a key piece of the puzzle.

> An objective look at the community can give us a whole new insight into where God has called us to lead.

The three main areas of insight, where you are now are:

1. **Current Leaders** – Who are your current leaders? How did they get into their leadership positions? How long has each leader in your church held some form of leadership position? What does the makeup of your current leadership team tell you about the process of leadership development currently in place in your church? Without using people's names, describe each of the leaders in your church based on their personal demographics (age, gender, race, household income, etc.). Be as complete as possible. Compare your overall leaders to your community. How well does your leadership team match the mission field?

2. **Mission Field** – What is the makeup of your community? Be sure to look at key areas such as population

trends, average age, single parents, white collar vs. blue collar, average household income, and the percentage of people in each generation. What does the data and statistics about your community tell you about what impacts leadership in your church? How is the present-day situation around your church impacting leadership development in your ministry?

3. **Church Situation** – Where is your ministry today? Where are you seeing fruit, and where is it time to prune? What are the top challenges you and your leaders are facing today in your church? What challenges do you feel least prepared to tackle as a leadership team?

The current church situation piece is very important for all of the following sections we cover in creating a leadership pathway for your church. In many organizations, churches included, leaders often find themselves putting out fires. We go from putting out one fire to putting out another fire. Often, we end up putting out the same fires over and over again. As leaders, we need to intentionally take time to determine what is causing those fires. This is a main component of the overall leadership development process. The general concept is closely related to how Ronald Heifetz and Marty Linsky refer to "getting off the dance floor and getting on the balcony" in their book, *Leadership on the Line: Staying Alive through the Dangers of Leading.*[1]

Here are a few suggestions for you and the small team you are working with to help gain insight into the true current situation in your church:

---

1 Heifetz, Ronald and Marty Linsky. *Leadership on the Line: Staying Alive through the Dangers of Leading,* Harvard Business Review Press, 2002, p. 53.

> Remember, it is NOT about the numbers. It is about what the numbers are telling us.

• Look at the past twenty to thirty years of statistical data about your ministry. We have found it very helpful to create graphs where possible in order to take what can be a lot of numbers and turn it into a more visual presentation. Five key areas to look at are 1) membership; 2) average worship attendance; 3) baptisms—all types; 4) professions of faith—all types; and 5) removed by death—those members of the church who have passed away. There are many other areas you might review. These are just the top five we have used with church leaders. What trends do you see? What is the information telling you once you back away from today and are able to see the forest for the trees? Remember, it is NOT about the numbers. It is about what the numbers are telling us. Indicate on the graphs any major challenges in the church and any changes in pastors or other key leaders. Is there any type of correlation between leadership changes, conflicts or challenges, and the areas you are reviewing?

• Where is your church today on the church life cycle? There are many versions of the church life cycle available and many resources for how to understand and utilize the tool. We are not advocating any particular version or resource. We encourage you to do a little online research and find one that speaks to you and your church. Then take some time to share it with your whole leadership team and determine as a group where you feel your church is today on the life cycle. Some of the factors which influence where a church is on the life cycle are mission and vision focus, clear discipleship process and relationship emphasis, programs and ministries designed to grow disciples, and a structure which supports but does not drive the ministry.

• Where does it hurt? What are the current leadership challenges you are facing today in your church? Imagine a church doctor came to visit you and they started poking around and asking you lots of questions to determine the health of your leadership ministry. What are the top three or four things they would discover and write a prescription to address?

As disciples of Christ, we know that as long as we are on this side of heaven we are never finished growing as a disciple. No matter how long we have been on the journey, no matter where we are currently, there are always steps ahead of us. The same is true for us as leaders. True leaders never stop learning and growing. Like discipleship, no one can do it for us. We must take ownership and initiative. However, just like there is no such thing as a "Lone Ranger" disciple, leadership development is a team effort. While the leader him/herself takes ownership and initiative, the church plays a part by providing resources, encouragement, direction, and support. The third player in leadership development, as in discipleship, is the Holy Spirit. God's Spirit guides us and surrounds the whole process leading us ever forward.

Before we go any further on the journey of creating a leadership pathway for your church, we would like to share with you a few critical elements concerning church leadership which will guide our entire process.

1. We believe that leadership is a spiritual gift and something everyone can learn. While some people in our church will have the spiritual gift of leadership, we believe that serving in some form of leadership should never be limited to only those who are gifted in that area.

2. Leadership in the church flows out of our discipleship. Leaders must focus first on growing as a follower of Christ, then focus on growing as a leader. The book, *Stride Participant Book: Creating a Discipleship Pathway for Your Life* by Mike Schreiner and Ken Willard is a good resource to help your leadership team grow first as disciples.

3. Like disciples, leaders are never done growing as leaders. We are called by God to grow all of the gifts given to us. Intentional leadership development, like intentional discipleship, must be a part of all church ministry.

4. Churches need servant leaders who will follow the example of Jesus. There are many types of leadership in our world today. Our churches need to have leaders who are not focused on themselves or on their particular areas of ministry or preferences, but on serving others and giving God the glory.

5. Servant leaders help the church fulfill its mission to make disciples of Jesus Christ for the transformation of the world (see Matthew 28:18-20). When a church gets leadership right, they are focused first on making disciples of Jesus and growing God's Kingdom here on earth.

6. God has provided every church and ministry with exactly the resources, including leadership, needed to

make the difference God is calling you to make in the next chapter of your life. Our role is to be good stewards and to grow those resources.

7. The local church is the place where God's mission in the world takes place. These local churches are also uniquely positioned to provide support and hope to the communities they serve. The future of the local church and their communities rests primarily on the leaders serving there.

8. When local church leaders grow and develop, all ministries in the church are positively impacted and this will spill over into the mission field.

9. Leaders learn best from other leaders. Yes, leaders tend to learn from just about everyone in a wide variety of areas. But they learn best about leadership from other leaders. These leaders will seek out a coach, a mentor, or just someone who is a little ahead of them as a leader to learn and grow their skills.

10. Leaders learn how to translate everything they encounter and filter it into the context where they are serving. A strong leader can read a book that seems to have nothing to do with their current situation and still find lessons they can apply. They intentionally look for and discover something of value in every situation.

Once you feel confident about your leadership hindsight (where you have been) and your leadership insight (where you are now), then it is time to focus on the foresight component or where you are going with church leadership development. That is the focus of our next chapter.

Before you move on, we encourage you to spend a few minutes now to answer the following questions:

What was your key learning concerning the history, or hindsight, of your church leadership development?

What was your key learning concerning the current situation in your church?

What did you learn about your community or mission field? How do you see that information influencing your leadership development process?

What leader has influenced you the most in your own leadership? What might they say to you now as you embark on growing church leaders?

Prayer

Lord, we are humbled that you have called us into leadership in your church. We are thankful for the ways you have gifted us and for those leaders who have come before us on this journey. We pray for your Spirit to guide our paths and to give us all we need in order to equip ourselves and other leaders so that we may grow your Kingdom here on earth. Amen.

CHAPTER FOUR

Leadership Development Approaches

To aspire to leadership is an honorable ambition.

1 Timothy 3:1, NEB

If your actions inspire others to dream more, learn more, do more and become more, you are a leader.

John Quincy Adams

What is leadership? There are many wonderful definitions of leadership. Every leadership book and every leader seem to have a slightly different definition of what a leader is as well as what is leadership. While not a church organization, we like the definition used by the Ken Blanchard Companies, "Leadership is the capacity to influence others by unleashing the potential and power of people and organizations for the greater good."[2] When we refer to leadership throughout this book, the definition above is what we are using. We realize this definition might not be your favorite or capture what leadership is for you and your church. If so, take some time with your leadership process team to come up with

---

2 http://kenblanchard.indiatimes.com/ignite.html. Accessed October 14, 2019.

your own definitions of a *leader* and *leadership*. Then use those definitions and descriptions as you continue your work.

Leadership Roles

No matter the size of your church or organization, leadership is important to the fruitfulness and vitality of the ministry. This is just as true in volunteer-based organizations such as local churches or service groups as in businesses or for-profit companies. There are three different types of leadership roles in an organization which may be performed by multiple individuals or by one person wearing multiple hats:

- **Supervisor** – This is the first level of management. At this level, they are concerned with encouraging the members of a group or team to contribute positively toward accomplishing the organization's mission, goals, and objectives. What examples come to mind in your church? (Examples: Sunday school teachers, small group leaders, hospitality team leaders, etc.)

- **Manager** – People at this level control and are responsible for the activities and assets of an organization. They ensure that the organization stays focused on its purpose and mission. They manage resources such as people, finances, facilities, etc. and work to achieve tasks and maintain the organization. What examples come to mind in your church? (Examples: director of Christian education, director of music, finance chairperson, trustees' chairperson, pastor/parish relations chairperson, etc.)

- **Leader** – A person who takes the organization from

where it is today toward the future (vision) in order to achieve its collective potential. What examples come to mind in your church: lead pastor, executive director of arts, administrative board chairperson, lay leader of the church, etc.?

> A healthy ecosystem is always described as in balance and interconnected.

A healthy ecosystem is always described as in balance and interconnected. Each part of the environment has a specific role and purpose that is necessary to the whole. For example, the soil must provide nutrients to plants, water must hydrate the soil, and the atmosphere must be clean for growth to happen. These basic elements are essential and must be accounted for. All organizations need to have each of the above-named roles in place, and you have most likely found yourself playing each role at some time during your career.

People and organizations struggle when a person should be performing one role and they are actually doing a role one or two levels below where appropriate. For example, a person who is promoted to the director of Christian education position in a church but they spend most of their time teaching a Sunday school class because that is what they are most familiar with and comfortable doing. Have you ever seen a situation like that play out in your church? The need for different levels of supervision, management, and leadership dates back to biblical times. Moses was trying to do everything himself when his father-in-law, Jethro, gave him some great advice!

Moses' father-in-law said to him, "What you are doing isn't good. You will end up totally wearing yourself out, both you and these people who are with you. The work is too difficult for you. You can't do it alone. Now listen to me and let me give you some advice. And may God be with you! Your role should be to represent the people before God. You should bring their disputes before God yourself. Explain the regulations and instructions to them. Let them know the way they are supposed to go and the things they are supposed to do. But you should also look among all the people for capable persons who respect God. They should be trustworthy and not corrupt. Set these persons over the people as officers of groups of thousands, hundreds, fifties, and tens.

Exodus 18: 17-21

Levels of Leadership

In addition to the types of leadership described above, each organization will usually have people at various levels of leadership. Building on the writings of Ken Blanchard and others in the books *Leadership and the One-Minute Manager* and *Lead Like Jesus*, these are four levels of leadership within most local churches:

1. **Potential Leaders** – These are people who have never led anything, inside or outside of the church, but they show the gift of leadership and/or they are demonstrating an interest in leading. They are looking for opportunities to dip their toe in the waters of leadership without a major commitment. These individuals need the basics of leadership. They will typically respond well to encouragement, clear direction, short term goals, and structured follow-up. Too much responsibility or too large of a commitment

could push them away.

2. **New Leaders** – They are in their first leadership position in your church, and maybe their first leadership position anywhere. They are often very motivated to lead, but they don't know what they don't know. Leaders at this level will usually respond well to mentoring by a more experienced leader. We need to help them grow into a servant leader by becoming a leader like Jesus.

3. **Existing Leaders** – These individuals have experience leading in multiple types of teams and situations. They are usually capable of working on their own with little or no supervision. We need to challenge them to continue growing their leadership skills and look for ways to expand their influence. These leaders need a coach approach to their supervision with supportive behaviors and less direction.

4, **Seasoned Leaders** – In most organizations this is the top 10 percent of leaders. They have clearly demonstrated exceptional leadership skills in a variety of settings and situations. We need to provide them with opportunities to share what they know with others. (See mentoring new leaders above.) They need challenging assignments along with new networking and learning opportunities, which may be outside our normal areas of resources. The key with these leaders is delegation. Given a clear goal, they will most often find their own way to achieve that goal.

We are sharing the different leadership roles and the levels of leadership with you now because they should both play a part in your overall leadership development process planning. The leadership roles are important for you to remember because people in different roles will automatically filter everything they receive through the lens of those roles. For example, a small group leader and an associate pastor who both attend the exact same leadership event will likely have very different learnings from that training. The same is true with individuals who are on different levels of leadership. This does not mean you will need to provide for all possible combinations of leaders, it just means you need to factor this into your planning and understand how leadership roles and levels will influence each person's perception of the training.

Often in our work with churches we encounter people who are leaders in some type of leadership position, but do not see themselves as a leader. The reasons for this are numerous. As you and your team embark on this journey to create a leadership pathway for your church, you should remember that there is a good chance that some of the people you consider a leader may not see themselves as a leader. They may need a nudge along the way to get them to engage in your leadership development process. We have included a listing of common leadership positions in churches in Appendix One with the intention to get you thinking beyond the obvious leaders in your church.

Leadership Development Approaches

There are several popular approaches for organizations and churches to take when it comes to leadership development. The following are just a few of the ones we have seen over the years. As you read each of the different approaches, think about where you might have seen this approach taken in your experience and what might have been the reasons behind that approach. We would also encourage you to consider both the perspective of the church or organization employing each approach and the participant who is on the receiving end of each approach.

The first type of leadership development is what we refer to as the **Random Approach**. An image for this approach would be a pair of dice.

This is when an organization seems to do leadership development haphazardly and choses topics or competencies based on what is "hot" at the moment or what might be available and/or within the budget. This approach is similar to how migratory birds pick up and drop seeds, spreading them far and wide. Here are some examples of what an organization might do using the random approach:

- A well-known author is in town promoting a new book. We can get discount registrations at another church in town if we book ten or more people.

- Everyone in our conference has been talking about the book *Canoeing the Mountains* by Tod Bolsinger. Let's all read that book and discuss it at our next meeting.

- The district is bringing in a leadership speaker for the next meeting. Let's all register for that workshop.

None of these are "bad" due to the fact that any leadership development is typically better than none at all. In fact, there is a very good chance that some elements of this approach will meet at least some of your leaders right where they are and help them grow as a leader in your church. When I (Ken) play golf and make a rare good shot I will often say, "Even a blind squirrel finds a nut sometimes!" The challenge with this approach is that the organization is leaving a lot to chance and it will often feel very random to the leaders involved. Similar to migratory birds, it is difficult to see the effects of the seeds planted, but it can still cause new growth. We have seen where this approach is employed leaders will often perceive that there is no leadership development at all taking place because of the randomness. Without a clear plan, we are going in too many different directions to build up any momentum or really grow our leaders with intentionality. Ultimately, this approach to leadership development will always fall prey to the "tyranny of the urgent" and continue to be a low priority in the organization.

The second type of leadership development is what we refer to as the **Pain Approach**. This is the "tell me where it hurts" type of leadership development. The image for this approach would be a bandage.

In this situation the organization is using leadership development to try and "put out fires" or to address performance and/or some type of outcome issues. Here are a few examples of what a pastor or leader might say to better explain this approach:

- "Too many people on our team are coming in late! We need to do some time management training!"

- "None of our small group leaders are turning in their attendance reports correctly. Let's make them all attend a mandatory accountability training workshop."

- "We are hearing a lot of complaints about the changes we made last month to our children's ministry check-in system. I think the team leaders need some change management training."

Like the Random Approach, none of these are in and of themselves "bad." One of the challenges here is that we may not be addressing the correct issue. Another challenge is that the training or leadership development is not some type of magic pill that will suddenly make everything okay. This is especially true with performance issues. Another consequence of this approach is that we could be sending a signal that the only time we do leadership development is when something goes wrong.

In the book *Gapology* by Mark Thienes and Brian Brockhoff, they share a process for ensuring you are addressing the correct issue in any situation. The short version is that anywhere you find a gap between what is expected or wanted and an actual result, we need to look closer to see which type of gap or gaps actually need to be addressed in order to effectively close the overall gap. A physical gap that exists for animals is a highway or other road. These thoroughfares keep animals from reaching needed food or water. To close these gaps, communities build literal bridges for animals to make it across dangerous roadway crossings so they can reach needed resources for their health and survival. When we address gaps, we literally build bridges from where we are to where we need to be. While this is much easier to explain in person or during a training session, the following is an example along with a visual of the concept.

Let's say no one in the church is inviting anyone new to come join them for worship. That would be the main gap – we want/expect everyone to invite their friends, family, neighbors, etc. to come to worship, but the actual result is they are not doing it.

The first gap is the **Knowledge Gap** and it focuses on **The What** and **The How**. This is the space between not knowing what to do, or how to do something and knowing what to do and how to do it. This gap is typically closed with teaching or training. The question to ask is, "Do they know how to invite someone to worship?" In theory, this gap can also be closed by bringing in people who already know how to invite. This is the "talent" component. We need to be confident that the Knowledge Gap is closed before we move any further.

The next gap is the **Importance Gap** and it focuses on **The Why** and **The When**. This is the space between knowing what and how to do something and knowing why and when to do it. This gap is closed with communication, clarification of expectations, and helping people prioritize. The questions to ask here are, "Have we effectively communicated to everyone how important it is for them to invite people to worship? Do people know when it is most effective to invite new people to worship? Have we clarified our expectation that all members will invite unchurched people to worship? With all we are asking people to do in our ministry, what level of priority do people see inviting new people to worship?"

The final gap is the **Action Gap** and it focuses on **The Choice**. This is the space between knowing something is important and actually taking action. This gap is closed with accountability, commitment, and culture. Accountability in this case, and throughout all ministry, should be positive. What are the positive consequences of inviting someone new to worship? How can we hold people accountable in love to inviting unchurched people? Think celebrations, not punishment. Commitment comes from within a person. We cannot make someone committed to anything. However, we can recognize and encourage commitment. The most powerful element of all these is culture. (We will talk more about culture in another chapter.) If a church has a culture of inviting people to worship, then the majority of people will want to join in and be part of that group. New members of the church will also be more likely to follow the culture than anything said from the pulpit or printed in the bulletin. People always have a choice in taking action or not taking action. Our role as leaders is to help our congregations see the best choices of action for God's Kingdom and our mission. The image below is a graphic representation of the overall *Gapology* concept. Again, this is just the short version of the concept, our intention is for you to consider these elements as you are creating a leadership pathway for your church.

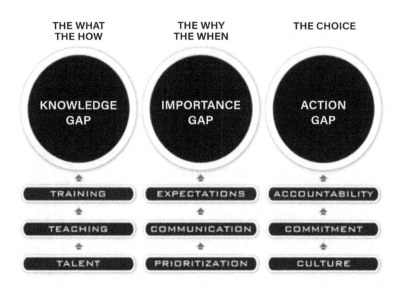

The third type of leadership development is the **Organizational Approach.** This is the "We're in charge, so we know best" approach to leadership development. An image for this would be a large arrow pointing downward.

In this scenario the senior leader(s) decide what competencies all of the leaders in the organization need to be proficient in for the organization to be successful. In some cases, this is done by looking at the top leaders in the organization and trying to determine the skills and competencies they have which are making them successful.

There are some benefits to this approach. First, the organization can focus all of their leadership development on a few key competencies. Second, communication and evaluation of performance is improved due to this heightened focus. And finally, this is actually a great way to launch a new leadership development initiative because of the factors listed above. We will talk more about leadership competencies later in this chapter. One of the main issues with this approach is that many leaders do not appreciate a top-down approach to their development.

The next type of leadership development is the **Individual Approach**. As the name suggests, this approach is focused on and driven by each individual leader. An image for this would be a large arrow pointing upward.

All development is catered to their specific wants and needs. In many situations the individual leaders will take one or more tests or surveys designed to show where they are strong and where they are in need of work. Each leader then works with someone like their supervisor, a human resources representative, a pastor, pastor-parish relations committee representative, or other person who can provide resources and direction for their personal leadership development. Here is an example of a servant leadership self-assessment survey each leader might take in order to identify their areas of focus (survey found on following page).

Read each area and then honestly assess yourself on a scale of 1 to 5.

1 = rarely 2 = sometimes 3 = often 4 = frequently 5 = consistently

_____ 1. I receive constructive feedback from others without becoming defensive or challenging.

_____ 2. I focus on preparing and empowering others to succeed in their roles.

_____ 3. I am preparing a successor to take my place of leadership when my season is complete.

_____ 4. I am comfortable letting God be the leader and for me to take the role of a servant.

_____ 5. When treated like a servant, I respond like a servant without question or insult.

_____ 6. I strive to lead not out of fear or to create a sense of fear in those I lead.

_____ 7. When I encounter a negative situation or person, I work to make everything better.

_____ 8. I recognize and accept people for their uniqueness and try to understand their point of view.

_____ 9. I listen more than I talk. When others speak to me, I listen actively, not waiting to speak.

_____ 10. When things go well, I celebrate the work of others. When things go badly, I look in the mirror to focus on what I could have done better.

A leader might take the above self-assessment and then determine themselves how they would like to proceed based on their view of their servant leadership skills. The church or other organization would be there to help guide them toward possible resources (coaching, training workshops, etc.) but would still allow the individual leader to guide and take ownership of their own development. This approach is by far the favorite of many individual leaders, but can be a real challenge to manage and deliver. Another challenge with this approach is that there is no foundation for leadership development so leaders who are not focused on their own development will find themselves falling behind or getting stuck.

The next leadership development approach is called the **Strengths Approach**. This is based on the work of the Gallup organization. They have many great resources related to this approach. Two that we would recommend are *StrengthsFinder 2.0* by Tom Rath and *Now, Discover Your Strengths* by Marcus Buckingham and Donald O. Clifton. The short version is that from the research of the Gallup organization, the area most people have the greatest potential for growth is where they are already strong. The key is to not let your areas of weakness trip you up, but also not to throw too much time and effort into trying to grow those weak areas either.

In addition to their books, Gallup also has a very good online survey designed to identify areas where a person is the strongest. These resources and the online survey have been used by numerous businesses, churches, and other organizations for many years. Many Christians find a clear connection to how Gallup focuses on a person's strengths and how churches should focus on where God has uniquely gifted each person with spiritual gifts.

Leadership Competencies

> Leadership competencies are skills and behaviors which contribute to the success of both the individual and the organization.

We have mentioned competencies a couple of times already in this section. Leadership competencies are skills and behaviors which contribute to the success of both the individual and the organization. There are almost as many possible competencies as there are definitions of leadership. Listed below are a few key competencies:

- Coaching skills
- Facilitating change
- Growing new leaders
- Decision making
- Risk taking
- Communication skills
- Building trust
- Valuing diversity
- Planning and organizing
- Accountability
- Emotional intelligence
- Time management
- Inspiring others

- Managing conflict
- Delegating Responsibility
- Emotionally healthy
- Leading like Jesus
- Servant leadership
- Cultural proficiency
- Faith sharing/evangelism
- Leading productive meetings
- Inspiring others
- Methodist/Wesleyan ethos
- Perseverance
- Strategic planning

What other leadership competencies would you add to this list? Churches and organizations will often create a master listing of competencies they feel each leader should have in order for individuals to be successful in their roles and to ensure the organization achieves its mission and goals. We believe that any discussion about leadership development in churches should include a focus on competencies. Clearly defining which competencies are most important can enable your church to better determine which resources are appropriate and specifically what you are hoping to achieve through your leadership development initiative. Like an ecologist evaluates the markers of a healthy ecosystem to determine environmental health, a leader is not evaluated by tasks completed. Instead, they are evaluated by what markers they are reaching on the way toward the difference they are called to make and what competencies get them to that difference in the overall environment.

Before jumping right into the next chapter on creating an intentional leadership pathway for your church, we encourage you to pause and reflect on everything we covered in this chapter. Take a few minutes to answer the following questions:

What definition of leadership are you going to use in your ministry?

When you refer to "leaders" in your church, what types of positions are you including?

How many leaders do you currently have in each of the levels of leadership? How will that influence your plans for leadership development?

Which type of leadership development approach has your church been using? Why? What results have you seen?

What leadership competencies do you feel your leadership development process will need to address?

Prayer

Lord, we are thankful for the leaders you have provided to this ministry in the past, today, and the ones you will provide as we live into your future. Give us the ability to see how you have gifted leaders, and others, all around us for the work of your Kingdom. We pray that we are good stewards of the people and other resources you have generously provided to us. Amen.

CHAPTER FIVE

Creating Your Leadership
Development Pathway

*Let's not get tired of doing good, because in time
we'll have a harvest if we don't give up.*

Galatians 6:9

*The three great essentials to achieve anything
worthwhile are, first, hard work; second,
stick-to-itiveness; third, common sense.*

Thomas A. Edison

We believe the best approach for leadership development
in a church or other organization is a combination of several
of the approaches we just reviewed, accompanied with an
intentional overall strategy. After the Cuyahoga River fire,
a specific plan was developed to help make the river healthier. In an NPR interview, Jane Goodman, the head of the
Cuyahoga River Restoration said, when asked about the
intentional plan to restore the Cuyahoga river, "The first
job was to clean it up to a point where life could happen and
persist."[3] The plan worked because there was a target they

---

3 NPR.org. "How Ohio's Cuyahoga River Came Back to Life 50 Years After it Caught on
Fire" https://www.npr.org/2019/06/18/733809317/how-ohios-cuyahoga-river-came-back-
to-life-50-years-after-it-caught-on-fire. Accessed October 14, 2019.

were striving to reach. Just as the river, a church must also focus on the organizational goals and needs PLUS a focus on the goals and needs of the specific area where the leader is working or serving PLUS a focus on the goals and needs of the individual leader. Here is an illustration of what that looks like:

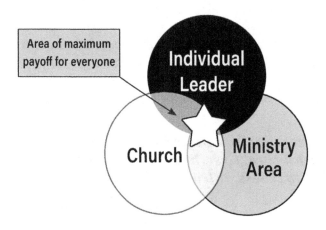

Let's take a closer look at this concept of determining the specific areas of focus for leadership development in your church. First, consider your overall ministry. Review the Pain Approach section we covered before. Where are you feeling pain in your leadership now? As you think about leadership in general throughout the church, what are the key competencies all effective leaders must have? Each leader is of course different, but as you look through the history of the church, what leadership trends do you find? The church circle in the image above represents the voice of your total church. Based on your insights, the team you are working with in this process, and the data you have

KEN WILLARD & KELLY BROWN

gathered, what skills and abilities do all effective leaders in your church need to possess? We encourage you to write these down. You do not need to use the image above, but you should create some type of master listing with three columns. The heading of one column should be "Church," the second column should say "Ministry," and the third column should read "Individual." The most critical skills and competencies for a leader in your church should go in the "Church" column.

Now consider each of the main ministry areas of your church. Some examples might include: children's, Sunday school, finance, trustees, worship, pastor and staff relations, and so forth. We would encourage you to not automatically assume you know what each ministry needs, but to actually have some conversations with each ministry leader or team. Ask them what specific skills, abilities, and competencies an effective leader in their ministry needs to have in order to ensure the fruitfulness of that ministry. One word of caution: as you ask the ministries throughout your church, they will often think about specific leaders either in the past or in the present. While that information is certainly helpful, you may need to ask additional questions in order to go deeper in order to find the information you need. For example, someone on a ministry team could say, "Bonnie was great at making decisions." An effective follow up question could be, "How did Bonnie's ability to make decisions impact the fruitfulness of your ministry?" The point is to intentionally connect the skills and abilities of past or current leaders in the ministry to our process of leadership development. As you and your team identify these skills, abilities, and experiences you should record them on your

57

master listing in the "Ministry" column.

The third circle in the image and the last column on your list is for individual leaders. Here you are gathering the voice of each leader in your church. There are various ways you can go about doing this. The one we would recommend is a survey of some type. The survey can be done on paper – or online – or some combination of the two if you want. We encourage you to keep it simple in order to increase the likelihood your leaders will take the time to complete the survey. Here are some examples of questions you could ask on your survey:

- What skills, abilities, and experience have been most helpful to you in your church leadership roles?

- What competencies would you most like to grow and develop in the coming season of church leadership? (You may need to provide a listing of options or examples.)

- Which leadership courses would you be most interested in taking in the near future? (List a dozen or so examples of leadership courses you would be willing to provide. Use the information you gained from the "Church" and the "Ministry" sections to guide the course listing.)

- What else would you like to share with us concerning your leadership development? (It is always a good idea to provide at least one open-ended question so the participants can share information with you which you may not have specifically asked.)

The individual leaders should be able to complete the survey in less than five minutes. This will increase the number of responses you receive. In a smaller church, you may want to just create a one-page questionnaire and then have conversations with each of your leaders where you ask them the questions and record their answers. While you may not be able to obtain 100 percent participation from your leaders, we do encourage you to try to hear from at least a strong majority. The key findings from the survey should go on your master listing under the "Individual Leader" column.

> ...an organization should intentionally listen more to its individual people than it does to any ministry, department, or the senior leaders.

Once you have the skills, competencies, abilities, experience, courses, and so forth listed under each column on your master sheet, it is time to analyze the information. The first thing to look for are trends or similarities. While the words and phrases used might be different, look for anything that appears in all three columns. For example, several individual leaders may have indicated that they would like to improve their time management skills, ministry leaders may have talked about the need for leaders to be able to organize tasks and manage the calendar, and in the church column you may have felt that setting effective goals was a key skill for all leaders. It would be very appropriate at this stage to call all of those "time managements." You will have an opportunity later as you provide leadership training to ensure the more specific requirements are covered.

We would encourage you to add more weight to the "Individual Leader" column than you do to the other two columns. The reason for this is that an organization should intentionally listen more to its individual people than it does to any ministry, department, or the senior leaders.

By adding more weight to the individual response, you can avoid the feeling which occurs sometimes when people feel like training is being done "to them" instead of "for them." We are not saying you should only listen to the individual leaders. We are just encouraging you to not listen to all three areas equally. While there is no magic or correct percentage distribution, here is an example:

Church = 30%

Ministry Area = 20%

Individual Leader = 50%

There are two groups of leaders you will also need to factor into your leadership development plans. The first group consists of those people who are currently serving in some leadership role now in your church. The second group will be those people who are not currently serving in leadership roles, but will be doing so in the future. In some cases, they may already be attending the church, but in other cases they are not even connected to the ministry yet. The reason you need to consider both groups of leaders is that these two groups will engage differently with the leadership development pathway. The leaders who are here now can easily be identified and you will usually only need to communication with them once or twice to let them know your plans and how to engage in the leadership development process. Those who are not here yet are a little more challenging. While it might be easier to develop an "on ramp" for getting into the leadership development process, you will need a whole different strategy for communicating the pathway and their role in it to those not yet involved, than what you use for those who are already in church leadership roles.

The following are key components we encourage you to include in your leadership development process. While these components will look different in different churches due to many factors such as the size of the church, the current group of leaders, the culture of the ministry, location of the church, type of church, etc., we do feel every church can and should have each component in place. You will need to filter everything through the lens of your ministry. Throughout this section we are going to share a few examples from Morning Star Church. This is a very large church in the suburbs of St. Louis. The examples are not there for you to copy as you are not Morning Star Church. They are only being provided as a way for you to see some possibilities and to have something tangible to filter through the lens of your ministry.

First Component: Begin

Where does your leadership pathway start? Remember the two groups we mentioned before, the leaders who are here now and those who are coming? Your starting component will need to look a little different and be communicated a little differently to each of these groups. How will you communicate the overall leadership development process, your goals for developing leaders, and the expectations of each leader?

At Morning Star Church this component is a two-hour class taught by the senior and founding pastor Mike Schreiner. During this class, pastor Mike focuses on the following areas:

- How leading at Morning Star Church is an extension of the church's discipleship process.

- His beliefs about church leadership, along with Bible verses to support each belief, with a focus on servant leadership.

- There is a time of small group discussion focused on the following servant leader characteristics: active listener, commitment to the growth of others, empathy, healing, awareness, persuasion, vision, conceptualization, stewardship, and building community.

- Each leader completes a servant leadership self-assessment and shares with a partner.

- Using Bible verses as a guide, pastor Mike unpacks the following Christian leader qualities: 1) Fulfill our Godly mission; 2) Do God's work and develop God's people; and 3) Grow ourselves as servant leaders. This section ends with some practical examples of how leaders can demonstrate servant leadership.

- Leaders in the class then share their key learnings from the day, write out their next steps, and complete a short evaluation of the class.

- The Bible verse, *"All of you must put on the apron of humility to serve one another. For God resists the proud but gives grace to the humble"* (1 Peter 5:5, GNB) is read as a closing to the teaching time. Pastor Mike then tells the class that Christian leaders are the servants of the servants of God. Before ending with a prayer, the whole group reads out loud the Wesleyan Covenant Prayer.

What might this look like in your church? It can and should look very different than the example we shared from Morning Star Church. Over the years, we have heard from many churches who once a year will do some type of orientation class for all of their incoming leaders. While some churches tend to focus this time on the logistics of leadership in the church, when and where the committees meet, what reports are due and when, how to be reimbursed for expenses, etc., this can also be a time to start leaders on their development pathway. What would an investment in starting your leaders off on their journey look like in your church? How often do you envision holding this class? Once a year? Twice a year? When is the best time to hold this class? What will be the foundation of your leadership process? Before you go any further in this book, take a few minutes to answer those questions and begin to draft out an outline for the starting point class of your new leadership pathway. Hopefully, you are working through this whole leadership development process with a few other people. If not, this is the time to stop working on your own and to bring in two or three others who can help you on the journey. (Read Ecclesiastes 4:12 and follow that very good advice.)

Second Component: Baseline

What comes to mind when you read the word *baseline?* No, we are not talking about basketball. We are using the term baseline to refer to the minimum level of leadership knowledge you expect from everyone who holds a position of leadership in your church. Remember the competencies we covered earlier? Those competencies can be a very good guide in this component. While we would all love for each leader in our churches to be proficient in all of the competencies, and walk on water, we do need to narrow our focus down in order to create a workable baseline. Here is one way to narrow your list down to just a few. Gather the people who are working with you on creating a leadership pathway for your church, and maybe another one or two key leaders who can add to the wisdom of the group. Use a large white board or maybe several sheets of large flip chart paper and list out as many competencies or leadership skills you can think of as a group. Do not worry about the order or exact wording, as long as everyone understands the essence of each. Now each person gets to vote for their top three. One way to do this is that their number one choice gets three points, their number two choice gets two points, and their number three choice gets one point. Then total up the points for each leadership competency or skill. Now go back and look at the information you collected from individual leaders and church ministries to be sure you are hearing from everyone appropriately. Do not forget to add extra weight to the individual leader data. This should give you a clear picture of which ones are most important to everyone. Narrowing the list down to no more than three or four should be your goal.

Morning Star Church did this process and identified four topics: accountable leadership, conflict resolution skills, growing new leaders, and leading like Jesus. They then created a course called "The Leading Edge" where these four ninety-minute classes were taught to all church leaders. The last class included a church leadership covenant, which we will cover in another chapter. Each leader was also assigned a trained coach whom they would meet with in the weeks following the class. We will talk more about coaching in another chapter too, but right now it is important to understand that a key component of the coaching session was for each leader to map out their personal leadership development plan.

What should this component look like in your church? Which competencies, skills, or topics made the cut from your earlier activity? Before you start getting overwhelmed by this process or start thinking, *This is great for a large church, but will never work here!* we would like to share some best practices and suggestions with you. Most local churches are part of a larger group of churches – like a district in the United Methodist denomination – or have other churches located near them in the same community. You might explore the possibility of doing a joint leadership development process with one or more of the churches in your district or community. Maybe all of you settle on six leadership topics you want to teach with all of the leaders from several churches. You could meet once every other month at one of your churches for learning and growing opportunities. This is a great way to get out and see the overall mission field from a new perspective and learn from new people. Another advantage of this type of arrangement is that you and your leaders do not have to be experts on all topics. For example, you may want all of your leaders to take a class on time management but you do not really have anyone who is strong enough on that topic to teach other leaders. The church down the street might have the perfect person for that topic, but may also need you or one of your leaders to teach a leadership class where they are unable to find the right teacher. We are always stronger together. Another option might be to teach all of the classes with leaders in your church, but to space them out so you are only doing one each quarter of the year. You can do this! Focus on the possibilities and potential fruit for your ministry and the Kingdom. Do not listen to the voice telling you it will not work in your church. That is not God's voice.

Those two components—a beginning and a baseline—will be enough to get your new leadership development pathway off the ground. Now you need to create a process to keep it going. Before we get to the next stage, a word about church communications. In most churches, the majority of communication to the congregation is concerning an event. Check out some of the communication from your church over the

> Focus on the possibilities and potential fruit for your ministry and Kingdom.

last few weeks. Look at newsletters, emails, bulletins, etc., and see if most stories have a date associated with them in some manner. This is not a bad thing, but we do need to understand how we have conditioned our congregations. They now expect for everything to be connected with a date of some type and once that is past, we are on to the next event. Need an example of that conditioning? Think about the last time your church taught on or focused on the spiritual discipline of giving. We bet it was connected to a stewardship campaign of some type. What happened to financial giving once the campaign was over? Did it go back to the level it was at before the campaign? If so, then it was an event. People got excited, and they increased their giving for a goal. But once it was over, they went back to where they were before. They were *involved* but not *transformed*. To state the obvious, discipleship and leadership are not events. One of the most common challenges we have seen in churches who create a new discipleship or leadership pathway in their church is that they turn them into an event. Once the excitement of something new dies down people start saying, "That was great, what's next?" We share this with you now because the most challenging part of both discipleship and leadership development is that they are ongoing processes: the daily, weekly, monthly discipline to grow closer to Jesus as both a disciple and a leader.

This third component of growing into a fully devoted leader has three areas: **Belong, Become,** and **Bless.** We will look at each area separately and share some ideas and suggestions with you about what each area might look like in your church.

Belong

One way for leaders to continue to grow on their journey is to be in a community of leaders. While there are many ways this can happen, and many forms it could take for local church leaders, we are going to focus on just two of them. The first way for leaders in your church to be in a community of leaders would be to utilize your current teams or committees. This does not require creating anything new or adding new groups to your existing structure. However, it may require transitioning into a new way of holding your leadership meetings. While this can be accomplished with any team or committee in the church, we are going to use the main church leadership team as an example. (In many United Methodist churches this is called the Administrative Board.) Look at the last few agendas for this team. What might it look like to start these meetings with a few minutes of discipleship followed by a few minutes of leadership development? If these are the leaders guiding your church into God's future for the ministry, then that might be a good investment. You might consider having everyone read a leadership book and then discuss a chapter or two each time you meet. If you are intrigued by this, we highly recommend the book *Mission Possible: A Simple Structure for Missional Effectiveness* by Kay Kotan and Blake Bradford. This fits closely with the process of loving, learning, and leading being used by Spiritual Leadership, Inc. (or SLI) in many United Methodist conferences.

Another way to create a community of leaders as part of your ongoing leadership development process is to bring together a group of leaders specifically for this purpose. Many United Methodist Church conferences have used some version of a process known as the Healthy Church Initiative. Much of this process was based on the work of Dr. Paul D. Borden and his books, such as *Direct Hit: Aiming Real Leaders at the Mission Field*. In all of the versions of these processes, there is an element of continuous leadership development. Groups are formed with either clergy, laity leaders, or some combination of the two. These groups meet every month or so, read books together, and determine how to best use what they are learning back in their own churches. While there is often a curriculum developed specifically for this purpose, that is not always necessary. These communities of leaders are led by a facilitator who is more of a guide than a teacher. The leaders learn and grow together, they share life with each other in times of prayer and fellowship, and they hold each other accountable to the commitments they share with each other to implement what they are learning in their churches. These communities share a lot in common with the leadership bands used by John Wesley.

Depending on the size of your church, the number of leaders who want to be in a community, and other factors, you might choose to have one or more of these leadership groups in your church or you may want to include leaders from other churches in your area. Either way, the following are a few best practices for you to consider concerning these groups:

- Keep the number of people in each group small. Somewhere between six and twelve people is a good rule of thumb. Less than six, and the learning from each other becomes limited. More than twelve, and some people will have a challenge having their voice heard.

- Be clear about the purpose of the community. The goal should be to learn and grow together as leaders and to implement what they are learning in their churches. These are not book clubs or "whine and cheese" gatherings. Set the bar high at the start and encourage an environment of accountability.

- Each leadership community should create a covenant for their time together. (We will cover covenants in more detail in the next chapter.) Let them establish their expectations for each other and their time together.

- Do not forget the logistics of these sessions. If the participants in these groups are going to read a book together each month or so, who will pay for those books? This may not seem like a big deal to you, but it can be an obstacle for some leaders. We have found it best to address issues such as book costs, travel reimbursement, meeting space, coffee and snacks, etc. up front so these logistical issues do not take up valuable time and focus later. In some cases, the church, the district, the conference, or even a generous member of the church may be able to pay for some or all of the books and other materials.

- Have a start and an end date for the groups. We suggest that you not have any group run for over a year. This allows your leaders to engage for a while knowing that there is a clear finish. Some leaders may not mesh well with the whole group, but they might be willing to stick it out knowing there is an end date to the leadership community. Once the leadership learning group ends, allow a time of at least a month or more before you start up a new group. Give your leaders some margin and some space. When you start up a new leadership community, you may find that many or even all of the leaders sign up again. That is great! But you should still always have a start and an end date to the groups.

- These types of leadership communities are best done as a voluntary process and not as some form of mandatory sessions. You should encourage the leaders in your church to be in some type of leadership community, but not mandate it for everyone. Most leaders will look for these types of opportunities and will jump at being in a group with other leaders. However, we all have seasons in our lives and our ministries where this just will not work. We should respect those seasons for other leaders. Give them space. They will engage when the time is right.

Become

The second area of continuously growing into a fully devoted leader focuses on becoming a leader like Jesus. While this area may seem less structured than some of the others, be careful not to mistake that for a lack of intentionality. Becoming a leader like Jesus focuses on churches and individual leaders making intentional plans each year for leadership development opportunities. We will share some options and examples with you, but this is an area where each church needs to contextualize the leadership development process to your environment and ministry. The most important aspect of this is to not let your leadership development fall into the random approach.

> The Bible is the best leadership book ever written.

Before we get to the examples, this is a good place to pause and reflect on some basics of leadership in a local church. Growing leaders is important, but not at the expense of our true mission and purpose. All local church leaders should be:

- **Growing as disciples first.** Spending time in God's Word daily and growing in their reading and understanding of scripture. The Bible is the best leadership book ever written. Our leaders must not sacrifice their reading of the Good Book in order to read other books. Do not assume all of your leaders are reading the Bible every day. Talk about it and encourage them.

- **Growing as disciples first.** Spending time serving in the church and in the community. Leaders set the example. They are certainly using their gifts and skills in leadership, but they should also be serving as greeters, ushers, cleaning up after a meal, working the parking lot, vacuuming the floor, etc. Servant leaders walk the walk. Give your leaders opportunities to put a white towel over their arm and serve others. Do you want servant leaders? Are you looking for leaders who are already serving or are you just hoping that your leaders will serve?

- **Growing as disciples first.** Giving generously to the church and growing in their giving each year. All leaders and their situations are different, but what do you see when you look at their financial giving records? If they are not tithing yet, does it look like they are heading in that direction? Be sure your leaders understand that the tithe was never meant to be the "ceiling" of giving, but the "floor." Financial giving is an area of leadership development many churches are uncomfortable with, and thus neglect. Leaders need to set the example in many areas, including financial giving to the church. We recommend the book *Not Your Parents' Offering Plate: A New Vision for Financial Stewardship* by J. Clif Christopher as a resource for this area.

- **Growing as disciples first.** Attending church worship services each week unless working, sick, or out of town. The number of times "regular" attendees are in worship each month continues to drop in this country. Leaders should again be setting the example and not following this trend. Most leaders would appreciate a pastor saying this to them. It is always good to know the expectations.

- **Growing as disciples first.** Inviting their unchurched friends, neighbors, family, and coworkers to attend a church service. Leaders must have a heart for those who are not yet connected to a church. Our mission from Jesus is to make disciples. A major part of that mission is finding God's lost sheep and bringing them home (see Luke 15:3-7). How many unchurched people have your leaders invited to a worship service in the past year? Are they setting the example in evangelism or just going along with the crowd?

Leaders are disciples first. Look at what Jesus modeled for us as recorded in the Gospels. Christ clearly knew scripture, spent time in prayer, attended the synagogue, invited all types of people to follow him, talked a lot about money, and washed the feet of his disciples—a wonderful example of leadership for all of us to follow. In the United Methodist tradition, we have a membership vow which says, "I will support this church with my prayers, presence, gifts, service, and witness." How are your leaders living into that covenant vow they took before God?

Here are a few examples for your church to help its leaders continue to become like Jesus:

- Encourage leaders to read all they can about leadership. There are many wonderful Christian and secular leadership books. We have included a listing of our favorites in Appendix Two. You could share a listing of your favorite leadership books or maybe ask the church to purchase a leadership book for each new leader when they step into their role.

- Hold an annual leadership event in your church. This could be a time of learning and also a time of celebration. You could have dinner together on a Friday night, and maybe even honor a leader or two with some type of award. Saturday morning could be a time where you bring in a guest speaker. An event for leaders with a focus on growing their gifts could become a focal point for your whole leadership development process.

- Encourage your leaders to go where leadership is taught. There are Christian and secular leadership events being held each year all over the country. These are great opportunities for a group of your leaders to attend together so they can process what they are learning and find ways to apply that learning in your ministry. One advantage we have today is that many of these events are being transmitted live to other locations or made available in other ways so you might not even have to travel to attend. Not sure where to begin looking for these events? Check with your local chamber of commerce, public library, or judicatory leader's office. We are sure you will find many great options.

- Purchase some short videos on various leadership topics or take advantage of online sources such as YouTube, Ted Talks, or other resources. Show a video as part of your leadership meeting or other training events. Plan ahead so you can connect the video to your teaching, an issue before the leaders, or an opportunity which has presented itself. Be sure to never just show a video. Give the leaders time to process through discussion with a few good questions and be sure there is a clear connection to your context and ministry.

- Host a leadership retreat for leaders in your church, and maybe other churches in the area. Find an off-site location where everyone can unplug for a while and recharge their leadership gifts and their soul. Consider making this a time of both spiritual and leadership growth. We encourage you to bring in someone from outside your church to act as the facilitator and maybe the teacher so you can participate along with the group.

- Every two or three years you could have your leaders complete a 360° assessment. These tools will provide your leaders with constructive feedback from those they lead, other peer leaders, and anyone they report to or is at a higher leadership position in the ministry. While there are many organizations online who specialize in this type of tool, with a little research, even the smallest churches should be able to create something in-house to provide the same information. (Some of your leaders may have had a bad experience with these tools in the past where an organization misused the results or did not provide the necessary resources for leaders to grow their areas in need of improvement. So, you may need to walk slowly into this by having conversations before launching anything.) This is a wonderful tool when used correctly. Be sure you fully understand how to utilize this tool before you roll it out with your leaders.

Leaders are learners.

• Leaders are learners. They also love to learn about themselves. Your church might sponsor church leaders to complete one or more surveys designed to give leaders a new insight into their leadership style and themselves in general. Examples include Myers-Briggs, Gallup StrengthsFinder, and DiSC. As a bonus, these can be great team building activities when your leaders have an opportunity to share the results with other leaders.

Obviously, this is not a complete listing of all the things you and your leaders can do to continue becoming a leader like Jesus. Our intent was just to give you a few examples to get you thinking about new possibilities. No church can or should try to implement all of these. Start small and just pick the one you can do with excellence. Maybe your church is already doing one or more of these. If so, great! Look closely at how it is being done. Is it being done intentionally or just randomly? What is your next step in this area? What might you do next year to grow this area of leadership development?

Bless

The third area of growing into a fully devoted leader is to bless others through our leadership. All of this learning and growing as a leader is not intended to be just for our benefit. We need to be sure we are using our gifts and skills to lead something. Leadership is not about a title. Too often in the local church we are so focused on filling key leadership positions that we take our eyes off what is really important. This area is about fruitfulness, for your ministry and for the Kingdom.

> Leaders learn best from other leaders.

Here are a few examples of ways your church leaders can bless others with their gifts, skills, and experience:

- Provide mentoring to someone who is just starting out on the leadership journey. Leaders learn best from other leaders. In nature, this same type of connection is called a mutual symbiotic relationship such as between the plover bird and the African crocodile. The small bird picks food morsels from the crocodile's teeth as a meal. In return, the crocodile's mouth is free of infections and fresh. As a result of this exchange, both parties are healthier, and the ecosystem is healthier. The same is true with mentoring. Both the person being mentored and the mentor are benefited, and the church ecosystem flourishes due to the strength of its leadership. Partner up a more seasoned leader with someone who is new to leadership or maybe to someone you see the gift of leadership in but they have not yet found a way to use that gift in ministry. Here is a wonderful mentoring framework we learned from Community Christian Church in Naperville, Illinois and have used for many years:

o Do – You Watch – We Talk

o I Do – You Help – We Talk

o You Do – I Help – We Talk

o You Do – I Watch – We Talk

o You Do – Someone New Watches – We Talk

- This mentoring framework will work for just about any task or activity a leader does. The beauty is how simple and memorable it is. The most important component of each step is the "We Talk" part. This is best done with a series of short coaching type questions. Such as, "What did you notice?" "What would you have done differently?" and "What did you learn?" Try this model of mentoring the next time you make a leadership transition or have an opportunity for a seasoned leader to share with a new leader.

- Take advantage of leaders who have "rolled off" an official leadership position in the church or are maybe taking a season off of leaders for some reason. Ask them to fill in for other leaders in the church who are in need of a vacation or break of some type. In many churches, we only think about the leaders who are fully engaged by holding some type of official leadership role in the church. Many churches will also have at least a few leaders in the congregation who for various reasons are not holding an official position at this time. Encourage them to continue to bless others with their leadership skills, gifts, and experience by filling in for a leader from time to time who needs a short break.

- All communities are in need of strong leaders. Look for opportunities in your mission field where organizations are in need of leaders. We are not talking about positions of employment, but schools and other local community organizations who could use the skills, gifts, and experience God has so generously given to our ministry in our leaders. To state the obvious, this one will take a little work. It will require someone to actually talk to the organizations in the community, build a relationship with them, listen, and discover their needs. They may not even know what they need or be looking for help. A one-time, low commitment, type of service could turn into a wonderful blessing for both the community organization and your leaders.

These examples are only provided to help get you thinking about ways your leaders can bless others with their leadership gifts. We are sure you will be able to come up with many more specific to your ministry context. However, if you ever feel stuck in this or any of the other areas of **Become** or **Belong**, here are three suggestions to get unstuck:

1. Take it to God in prayer. Ask for the Holy Spirit to guide you and show you a new way. Search the Scriptures to see what other leaders did when they felt stuck. Do not keep it a secret. Tell others you are stuck and ask them to pray with you specifically for the option you are searching for in growing your leaders.

2. Partner with your leaders. This should never be a solo journey or meant to all sit on any one person's shoulders.

Pull together a small group of leaders you trust and share with them where you are stuck and ask them to brainstorm with you some new possibilities.

3. Get out of your box. It is hard to come up with something new when we are stuck in a rut. Most of us are creatures of habit and tend to do the same thing every day. Read the book *Get Out of That Box! Realizing Personal Potential & Enhancing Team Collaboration to Move Ministry Forward*[4] by Anne Bosarge and try out a few of the exercises she shares in the book.

Think back to the last time your church had to fill some key leadership positions. Many churches in the United Methodist denomination will use a committee known as the Nominations Team, which includes the pastor and several other members of the church. They will see which positions need to be filled and then try to figure out who would be the best fit for those open positions. (A church photo directory may also be in use at this point.) The best teams bathe this process in prayer and let God's Spirit guide them to discern the right people for each position. Too often, once the open slots are all filled, the team disbands for a year and only comes back together when there are new open positions to fill. Do you know what the official name of this team is in the United Methodist *Book of Discipline*? Check out paragraph 258.1. This is the committee on nominations and leadership development! Our point is, too many churches put all of their effort into filling leadership positions and little or no effort into growing those leaders or even setting expectations.

---

4 Bosarge Ann, *Get Out of that Box! Realizing Personal Potential & Enhancing Team Collaboratioins to Move Ministry Forward*, Knoxville: Market Square Books, 2018.

Our mission, as given to us by Jesus in Matthew 28:18-20, is to make disciples. This must be clear to all church leaders. We need to work with each leader so they can clearly see and articulate how the ministry they are leading is making disciples. A key component of this is for each leader and each ministry to have clear goals. How will they know they are being fruitful? What does fruit for the Kingdom look like in their ministry? Numbers and measurements are not the target, making disciples is the target. Numbers and measurements are just how we determine we are heading in the right direction.

The following image is what the leadership development pathway looks like at Morning Star Church. This is only being provided as an example. Your leadership pathway should certainly look different, because it will need to be specific to your ministry context. A graphic image is a nice way to show your process, but it should not be your focus as you work on creating a leadership pathway for your church. Focus on creating the process, and at some point, an image may develop and be helpful.

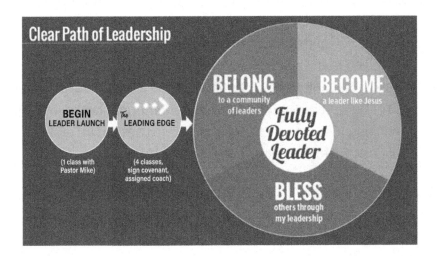

KEN WILLARD & KELLY BROWN

We have covered a lot of ground in this chapter. Now is a good time for you to pause and process the information and begin to look at how all of this will best translate into your ministry. While we have used labels such as: **Begin, Baseline, Belong, Become,** and **Bless,** you can and should come up with your own terms and labels for each leadership development element. The terms and labels are not important, as the focus should be on the elements themselves.

Before you go to the next chapter, take a few minutes now to answer the following questions:

What should the **Begin** element look like in your church? What is the appropriate way to engage your current leaders into the development process? What will be the on ramp for leaders new to your church?

What are the three or four **Baseline** competencies or topics you want to include in all of your leadership development? Who can you equip to teach each of these courses?

Who can you partner with on this journey to provide resources where you need them (another local church, your district or judicatory offices, or community organizations)?

What should **Become, Belong,** and **Bless** elements look like in your ministry? How can you fit each of these elements into the context of your church?

Prayer

Lord, we give thanks for the chance to grow closer to you each day. We see your hand at work all around us in nature and in each person we encounter. We pray now for all of the churches, pastors, and laity leaders who are on the path of leadership. May your Spirit be their guide as they grow themselves as your leaders so that we may reach ONE more for your Kingdom. Amen.

CHAPTER SIX

Covenants, Coaching, and Culture

He has brought salvation from our enemies and from the power of all those who hate us. He has shown the mercy promised to our ancestors, and remembered his holy covenant, the solemn pledge he made to our ancestor Abraham.

Luke 1:71-73

Coaching will become the model for leaders in the future . . . I am certain that leadership can be learned and that terrific coaches . . . facilitate learning.

Warren G. Bennis

Covenants

What comes to mind when you hear the word *covenant?* If you are married, you entered into a covenant with your spouse when you stood before God and repeated back the words spoken to you by a minister. If you are an ordained pastor, you entered into a covenant with God at your ordination service. If you are a member of a local church, you entered into a covenant with that church when you stood before God and agreed to the membership vows. In the United Methodist Church, that vow is to support the local church with our prayers, presence, gifts, service, and witness. Most definitions of the word *covenant* will speak to some type of agreement between two or more parties. A quick search on the website biblegateway.com shows more than 370 verses in the Common English Bible with the word covenant. This is clearly an important arrangement to God, and yet today we rarely speak of covenants in the church.

> Most definitions of the word covenant will speak of some type of agreement between two or more parties.

We would like to suggest for you and your leaders in the church to include a covenant as part of your ministry and work together. While the document itself and the creation of a covenant will not prevent bad behaviors or somehow magically guarantee that everyone gets along and works well together, it can be a way to get some important items on the table and add an element of clarity to your work.

Think back to the last church leadership team meeting. Your church may call that group an Administrative Board, an Administrative Council, or some other similar name. How did that meeting go? Were there any issues or challenges due to how the group interacts with each other or some other type of behavior? Now reflect back on these meetings over the past year or two. What trends, both good and bad, stand out to you concerning the way the group behaves and works together? Make some notes somewhere about the trends you are remembering. Now, let's go at this in a different direction. What do you expect from leaders in the church? Resist the first reaction of thinking about specific people or any forms of limiting thoughts. ("Ken's doing the best he can with his work schedule to attend our meetings" or "If I ask too much from our leaders they will stop serving" or "We've never done this before.") Start with the cleanest slate possible. Stay positive. Write down as many expectations as you can for yourself and other leaders in the church. Do not try to do any editing at this point, just capture everything that comes to mind. Finally, imagine you are launching a new church. God seems to be sending your church a lot of people with wonderful leadership gifts, experiences, and skills. As you are assembling the very first leadership team for this new church, you realize this is the perfect time to start off on the right foot with a clear leadership covenant. What would you want to include in that covenant? Add this to your notes from earlier. Now check out Appendix Three and compare your leadership covenant notes to the example we have provided.

There is one last important suggestion concerning leadership covenants. You would be wise to make this more of a collaborative process with your whole leadership team, rather than just walking in one meeting with the document completely filled out and asking everyone to sign it. Everyone, but especially a leader, likes to be part of this type of process and feel they have a voice in what they are agreeing to do and how they are to behave. Our advice is for you as the pastor or ministry leader to come up with your short list of non-negotiable items, and keep them in your pocket. Explain to the group what a leadership covenant is and ask for their input into creating one for your church. In many cases the process of creating the covenant as a group can be just as fruitful as the covenant itself, or even more so! As the group is creating the covenant, chances are good most or even all of your non-negotiable items will surface.

If not, then look for ways to insert them into the list where appropriate in the conversation. Not all at once. Once everyone is satisfied with the covenant, we recommend adding Scripture verses where appropriate to ensure a clear connection to the work being more about ministry together and not a list of "dos and don'ts." When the document is complete, a best practice is to make copies for all of the leaders and to have each person sign all of the copies. That way each leader will be able to keep a copy of the covenant with the total group's signatures. The intention of the leadership covenant is to be a tool to help ensure everyone is clear on the expectations and is living up to their end of the arrangement. It should never be used as an instrument of pain or punishment. Remember to intentionally refer back to the covenant from time to time and to update it each year or whenever the members of the group change.

> The ICF defines coaching 'as partnering with clients in a thought provoking and creative process that inspires them to maximize their personal and professional potential.

Coaching

The International Coach Federation defines coaching as "partnering with clients in a thought provoking and creative process that inspires them to maximize their personal and professional potential."[5] For our purposes in this book we are looking at coaching in two ways. The first

---

5 International Coaching Federation. https://coachfederation.org/code-of-ethics. Accessed October 14, 2019.

is as a skill we feel every leader should have in their leadership tool box. Coaching, at its most basic is about actively listening to other people, asking great questions, providing encouragement and support, bringing out the best in people, holding people accountable in a positive manner, and giving people space to grow. Skills that all of us as leaders need and most likely have room to improve on in our own leadership development. We encourage you to find opportunities to add coaching skills to your own leadership tool box as well as those of other leaders in your ministry. One way to do this is to attend a basic coach training event lead by a certified professional coach. While some organizations will provide this type of training for leaders in the business world, Coaching4Clergy and members of their faculty often provide this training for those of us in the church world. You can find out more on their website: www.coaching-4clergy.com. Here are three books on coaching we would recommend you and your leaders read:

1. *The Next Great Awakening: How to Empower God's People with a Coach Approach to Ministry*, by J. Val Hastings

2. *Coaching for Christian Leaders: A Practical Guide*, by Linda J. Miller

3. *Unlocking Potential: 7 Coaching Skills That Transform Individuals, Teams, and Organizations*, by Michael Simpson.

The second way we encourage you to look at coaching in the context of leadership development in your ministry is to provide opportunities for your leaders to engage with a coach. While it would be wonderful for all of your leaders to have an ongoing relationship with a professional coach, we understand how that might be asking too much for many churches. However, every church can support their leaders by giving them an opportunity to speak to someone in a coaching type situation about their personal leadership development. There are three things to look for in someone at your church who can do this type of leadership coaching: a great listener, a strong encourager, and a proven leader who has the ability to help other leaders grow their skills without telling them what to do. Think about the leaders in your church now. Who do you have who fits that description? We bet you have at least one person who can step into that role.

The following image is a tool we have found helpful in this type of coaching. Jesus was the best leader the world has ever seen. As we are all growing into the image of Jesus as disciples, we are also called to grow more like Jesus in our leadership. So, Jesus goes in the center of our wheel. The outer edge of the wheel can represent where we were when we started our leadership journey, or it can represent a novice in that particular leadership skill. Either way will work. Between the outer edge and the center are an infinite number of steps, even though we only show a few on the image. Each of us are somewhere between the outer edge and Jesus in each of the leadership skills. The eight leadership skills listed around the wheel are not meant to be the only leadership skills, or even the top leadership skills. Just eight most leaders need to, or want to, improve on when they are asked. Feel free to cross out any you want and replace them with other leadership skills you feel should be listed. Take a minute to make this personal by reflecting on the areas listed and indicate on the wheel where you feel you are today as a leader.

Leadership Coaching Wheel

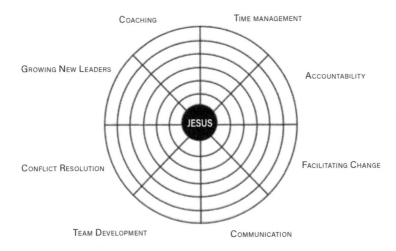

COACHING

TIME MANAGEMENT

GROWING NEW LEADERS

ACCOUNTABILITY

JESUS

CONFLICT RESOLUTION

FACILITATING CHANGE

TEAM DEVELOPMENT

COMMUNICATION

If we were coaching you using this tool, we might ask questions such as:

- Which leadership skills do you feel strongest in right now? Why?
- Which leadership skills would you like to grow in yourself in this season of your ministry? Why?
- What are your plans to grow that leadership skill? What else might you do to grow in that area?
- What would it look like to take one step forward as a leader in this season of your ministry?

The truth is that where we indicate we are in each of the leadership skills is not really important. What is important is for us to be active about taking a step forward. We must be intentional about growing as leaders. This type of coaching conversation and the leadership wheel are just tools to help us in that intentionality. Most leaders have been conditioned to focus on areas of weakness or areas in need of improvement. A good coach will encourage leaders to also look at areas where they feel the strongest. Those are often areas prime for a leap forward. This is closely related to the work of the Gallup organization and their StrengthsFinder books. As leaders, we do not want to let areas in need of improvement trip us up or cause us to not be fruitful in our ministry. However, areas where we are already strong may indicate the potential for a harvest a hundred, sixty, or thirty times what we sowed.

...the culture in our churches will usually determine how fruitful we really are in the end.

Culture

There is a phrase usually attributed to Peter Drucker, "Culture eats strategy for breakfast." This is certainly true in churches. No matter how great our plans are or how much time and effort we put into making changes or improvements, the culture in our churches will usually determine how fruitful we really are in the end. The polluting culture of the environment around the Cuyahoga River powerfully drove the end result of the river's death more than any plan to increase its vitality. No matter how much people wanted to catch a fish, unless sewers and steel mills ended their waste dumps, fish would never be caught. Culture is the most powerful force in most organizations, churches included. Not sure about that? Try changing the order of your worship service next week! Consider the story in Exodus about God's people leaving Egypt and journeying to the promised land. The trip took them forty years, even though they probably could have made the trip in forty days. Getting them out of Egypt was only the beginning. Changing their culture from being slaves to being the nation of God required getting Egypt out of them.

As you are working on establishing a leadership pathway for your church, keep in mind that part of what you are doing is creating a new culture of leadership development. Unless your church is a new church plant within the last year or two, you also need to realize that there is a current culture of leadership development already in place. So, as you are working on creating a new culture, you will need to be aware of the current one. How do you know what the current culture is in the church? Ask some people. Find a few leaders you trust to give you some honest feedback and ask them to describe the current leadership development process in your church. Resist the urge to correct them or add in any type of explanation or justification for how you currently are or are not developing leaders. Just listen for the culture to speak. The work you did earlier in the book about understanding where you are now can add to your understanding.

An analogy might be helpful. We both enjoy the sport of football. It is a great team sport and we enjoy watching all levels of teams. In the National Football League, the team who has the worst record for the year gets to pick first in the next draft of college players. The intent here is to create parity in the league by potentially having the best new players always going to the worst teams. However, there are some teams who just always find a way to win and other teams who are usually at the bottom. One factor in this is probably culture. The winning teams have a culture of winning and expect to win every game, no matter who they end up selecting in the draft. Some other teams may have a culture of losing and even when they select the number one player in the draft, that superstar is not enough by themselves to change the culture. The team continues to lose and everyone seems to have expected those results. Not a perfect analogy, but hopefully you see the point. Culture is a powerful force.

Think of a day in the future where your new leadership development process has been in place long enough to establish a culture of leadership development. What would that look like? How would you be able to see it and observe it in your ministry? What results or fruit would you expect to see? Imagine asking leaders around your church during this future to describe the church's leadership development process. What would they say? What words and phrases would they use? This is called crafting a vision.

> *"Vision without action is merely a dream. Action without vision just passes the time. Vision and action can change the world."*
>
> **Joel A. Barker**

By this point, we hope you have a clear picture of where your church is currently with leadership development. Crafting this vision of the future where there is a true leadership development culture in place can help you see a target to move towards. Creating yearly goals and action steps along the way, from where you are to where you want to be, will enable you to move into that preferred future.

In this chapter we have covered the topics of covenant, coaching, and culture. Hopefully you were able to see a clear thread connecting each of them and also connecting them to our overall focus on creating a leadership pathway for your church.

Before you move on to the next chapter, take a few minutes now to answer these questions:

What has been your experience with covenants like we covered in this chapter? How might a leadership covenant enhance the leadership development process in your church? When and how will you go about crafting a leadership covenant?

Have you ever taken any coaching skills courses or worked with a professional coach? Who in your leadership group can you equip to provide the coaching we talked about in this section? What is your next step to add coaching skills to your leaders' toolbox?

What is the leadership development culture in your church now? What are the next two or three steps you need to take in order to move that culture into the vision you have for a leadership culture? When will you take that first step? Who is with you on this journey?

Prayer

Lord, we are in awe of your creation around us. We read so many examples of your covenant of love in your Word and are encouraged that you never gave up on your people and are still calling us into covenant with you today. May we be worthy of your gifts of leadership and be a people today who partner with Christ in his new covenant. Amen.

Small Church Leadership

Consider a mustard seed. When scattered on the ground, it's the smallest of all the seeds on the earth; but when it's planted, it grows and becomes the largest of all vegetable plants. It produces such large branches that the birds in the sky are able to nest in its shade.

Mark 4:31-32

The world is moved along, not only by the mighty shoves of its heroes, but also by the aggregate of tiny pushes of each honest worker.

Helen Keller

How would you categorize the size of your church? Large, medium, small, something else? There are many lists out there in the church world which define what constitutes a large, small, or other size church. Most of them focus on average attendance in worship. We are not going to give you any size guidelines to work from. We are just going to let you determine yourself if you feel your church is "small" or any of the other sizes. This chapter is designed to help you translate and adapt everything we have been covering concerning leadership development and contextualize it

95

to your ministry setting. Following the Cuyahoga River fire's powerful plan of restoration, the strategies were adapted and applied to other Ohio watersheds based on their size and location. This led to the purification of not only the water, but the entire ecosystem. We feel strongly that churches of any size can and should be developing leaders. However, the manner in which churches develop leaders can and should look different based on many factors, including overall church size.

> We feel strongly that churches of any size can and should be developing leaders.

Considering our ongoing conversation about ecology, let's talk about farming for a minute. Throughout our country are many farms. Some of these farms are very large. They have hired employees who work the farm and they produce enough food sold through stores to feed thousands of people. Then there are the small farms. Usually these are a family focused first on feeding themselves and then when possible, they have some extras they can take to market and feed others. Obviously, these are just two examples of farm sizes. There are as many different sizes of farms as there are churches. A large farm is not "good" just because of its size, and a small farm is not "bad" either. The size of the farm will sometimes determine the type and number of crops and often the number of workers. We have been through many areas in our country where very large farms will be growing things like wheat or corn, and right down the street is a small farm with apples or cucumbers. They are not in competition with each other. The farmers understand their environment and what crops will grow best in that area. They also pay close attention to what people want to eat and changes in agriculture programs. The size of the farm does not determine how successful or healthy the crops will be or the farmers' return on their investments. Not a perfect analogy, but we hope you see a similarity to our conversation about leadership development in various size churches.

The following are suggestions for you and your church leaders to consider as ways to incorporate the information in this book and begin the process of contextualizing it to your ministry:

- Pray for a leader in your church during each worship service. Not as something new, just as part of your normal "prayers of the people" time. When you feel it is appropriate, add one leader from the community to your prayers.

- Contact a pastor or leader of another church in your area, even one not part of your denomination or group, and start a conversation about church leadership development. Buy them a cup of coffee and just talk. See where the Spirit takes the conversation. You may need to have more than one of these conversations and you may need to contact more than one church in the area in order to see fruit from your efforts. Do not rush it.

- Engage with your district, conference, or other type of office to see what resources might be available. There may be someone who can come to your church and meet with you and your leaders to help discern a process which fits best in your church.

- Take ONE step. Lay aside the whole talk of leadership development process and pathways and just focus on the one thing you and your leaders can do to grow this season. If reading and discussing a leadership book each month is too much, try just one this year. If creating leadership courses based on key competencies seems overwhelming, try gathering your leaders thirty minutes prior to a meeting one time to watch a short leadership video and then talk about how it might apply in your church.

- Find a larger church, of any type, in driving distance of your church and investigate what they are doing for leadership development. Build a relationship with them over time. Ask if your church might join them for one of their classes or when they bring in a leadership speaker. Chances are they would love to have other churches join them.

- Partner with other churches your size in the community to bring in a leadership speaker. While this might be too much for one small church, and some leadership speakers might not be willing to travel to just one small church, bringing together a few churches can be a benefit for everyone.

Picture a desert ecosystem in your mind. See the sand and the unique types of vegetation and animals God has created to live in that harsh environment. Now picture an ocean ecosystem. See the fish and other creatures, the plants and coral reefs, the ocean floor teeming with life that often looks so odd to our eyes. Now consider the ecosystem for the area of the country where you live. What types of plants, animals, and landscapes come to your mind? Which of those ecosystems would you call healthy? Is it possible that two extreme ecosystems, such as desert and ocean, can both be healthy even if they are so different? There is a quote often attributed to Albert Einstein, "Everyone is a genius. But if you judge a fish by its ability to climb a tree, it will live its whole life believing that it is stupid." Mega churches are not healthy merely due to their size. Small churches are not unhealthy just because fewer people attend their worship services. Both can be healthy, and both can be unhealthy. We believe one of the most important factors to a church living into its

> Do not let the attendance numbers of your worship service limit you or your impact for the Kingdom.

ministry potential is the church's ability to grow leaders. This can be done in a church of 40, a church of 400, and in a church of 4,000. It will just look different. Much the same as how different ecosystems can look different and all be healthy in the way God has designed and created them.

Churches of all sizes and types can and should be focused on growing leaders. Do not let the attendance numbers of your worship service limit you or your impact for the Kingdom. Leadership is not something only large churches should focus on. Strong leaders focused on God's mission for the church are even more critical in smaller congregations.

Before you move on to the next chapter, take a few minutes now to answer these questions:

What size category would you label your church? Why? Where does that label come from? How might your view of your church size limit your thinking about leadership development?

What is the ONE thing you are going to do this season to grow the leaders in your church? When will you have this completed? Who will you share this plan with to help hold you accountable?

Who can you talk to outside your church to partner with or provide resources for your church? When will you have that first conversation? What is your goal for that conversation?

Prayer

Lord, we wonder at the size of your creation: the mighty mountains towering over us and the creatures under our feet we cannot even see with our eyes. You created them all, great and small. Help us to see beyond the limits we place on ourselves and our ministry to truly see the potential before us when we place our trust in you. Amen.

CHAPTER EIGHT

Leadership Replenishment

Moses spoke to the Lord: "Let the Lord, the God of all living things, appoint someone over the community who will go out before them and return before them, someone who will lead them out and bring them back, so that the Lord's community won't be like a sheep without their shepherd.

Numbers 27: 15-17

Someone is sitting in the shade today because someone planted a tree a long time ago.

Warren Buffett

Have you ever found yourself struggling to fill a key leadership position in your church? Most of us have been there, some of us more times than we care to remember. There is no magic process or secret solution which will suddenly provide us all with a group of well-trained leaders sitting on the bench waiting for the perfect opportunity to fill our open positions. However, there are steps we can take to be better prepared for the leadership openings we will have in the future.

In the business world there is a process often known as *succession planning.* The Society for Human Resource

Management defines succession planning as "a focused process for keeping talent in the pipeline. It is generally a 12 to 36 month process of preparation, not pre-selection."[6] An organization engaged in succession planning is typically working to be proactive about who in their company can fill key leadership openings before those openings occur by providing training, mentoring, coaching, and new experiences to the appropriate individuals.

Let's look at this from a non-church example before we move back into the church world. Imagine a retail organization with many locations which is growing and expanding into new markets. Each local store has a store manager and two assistant store managers. A district manager in this company has a dozen stores located in several states. Susan, our district manager in this example, expects to open one new store in her district next year and would like to fill that position with one of her more experienced store managers. She also knows from past history that at least one of her store managers will retire or leave the company in the next 12 months. All of this means that she needs to prepare now to fill at least two or three store manager positions. Susan would like to promote from within if possible, so she will need to have a minimum of four to five assistant store managers ready to be promoted to store manager by the end of next year. She can now begin to review her list of assistant store managers to identify who has the potential for promotion and make plans for their leadership development. This brief overview will hopefully give you some basic

---

6 Society for Human Resource Management. "Engaging in Succession Planning." https://www.shrm.org/resourcesandtools/tools-and-samples/toolkits/pages/engaginginsuccessionplanning.aspx. Accessed October 14, 2019.

insights into the process.

Now let's switch over to the church world. Just to state the obvious, the process will look much different in our churches than it does in business organizations. However, there are some things we would be wise to take note of and adapt to our environments. The first is to be intentional. Leaders will leave, retire, rotate off, or be called to their heavenly home. It has happened before and will happen again. We need to anticipate and prepare for openings in our key leadership positions. Too often we in the church are being reactive instead of being proactive. We fill a key leadership position and then forget all about it until it is suddenly open again. Even if that "suddenly" was three years or more, and we knew the day it was going to come open again. In some cases, we may feel like planning for someone's replacement is somehow being disloyal or disrespectful to the leader who is currently filling that position. We must focus at least as much on the importance of the leadership role as we do on the person who is currently filling that role. Our mission is too important for us to allow any transitions in leadership to slow us down or cause us to stumble in our ministry. Certainly, we should honor the leader themselves, but we need to also honor the mission Christ gave us to do in our mission field. Be intentional in your ministry about creating a leadership replenishment system for key leadership roles.

The second learning from the business world of succession planning we should adapt to our ministry is to annually review each key leadership position and identify who in our church has the potential to fill each role. In many churches there is already an annual process of some type to name who is currently filling each key leadership position and to nominate people to fill any open positions. We would challenge you and your church to take the process you already have in place up to the next level by getting ahead of where you are now. In other words, don't just focus on the positions which are open. Review each key leadership position each year. Ask the following questions:

- How is the person who is filling this role doing now? Are there things we can do to help them improve and grow as a leader?

- If this person were to suddenly leave, who would fill this role? What do we need to do in order to prepare them for that situation?

- When this person leaves, (rotates off or steps down at some future date) who will fill this role? What do we need to do now in order to prepare them for that situation?

Before this becomes overwhelming, (too late?) take a deep breath and pause. Think clearly about where your ministry is now in this whole process of leadership replenishment. Now picture a future where the process is in place 100 percent and running like a well-oiled machine. What would be ONE step you could take in that direction this year? Just take that step. Too often we encounter a process like this and see the value, but never put it into place because we are trying to go from 1 to 100 in a week. Just take a step.

One way to gain support for this process of leadership

replenishment in your ministry is to involve each of the leaders who are filling those key positions. Be upfront with them and challenge them to pay an active role in the process. For example, when someone in your church accepts a nomination for a key position, (administrative board chair, trustees chair, finance chair, staff/parish relations chair, etc.) explain to them that one of their responsibilities is to identify and prepare their replacement. This is in no way intended to work around the church's current nominations team process, but to support it. Identifying and preparing someone for a position in the church should never be a guarantee that they will be offered that role. The intent is to be able to provide the nominations team with options to be included in their discernment process. We believe most nominations teams would welcome having additional options, especially when they have been trained and prepared for those key leadership positions. Using a typical three-year rotation, the first year or so a leader is in position they should be actively identifying people who have the potential for replacing them when they roll off their role. This would then provide them with one to two years for mentoring, training, coaching, and any leadership development the new person would need in order to be successful.

One more important part of this process is to look beyond the obvious choices. For example, too often a church will only look at people who are already on a team or committee when they are looking to replace the chairperson. The right person to chair your trustee committee might currently be serving in the children's ministry, finance, or as a greeter. We have worked with many churches where everyone on the finance team is either a banker, a CPA, or an accountant.

Those are great professions, but what is most important in church finances is a leader who understands the spiritual practice of generosity. It is usually better to find a leader who is tithing and either teach them what they need to know or surround them with experts, than to have a leader who is a financial expert and try to teach them about spiritual giving.

Now bring it all together. A white board or flip chart might be helpful for you and your team to see this process with names of people in your church. One way to do this is to draw out an organizational chart of the key leadership positions in your church. The image below is just an example. Your church will certainly look different. The image does not show reporting relationship, just an example of some key leadership positions in a local church. In a large church, some or all of these positions might be paid staff. In a smaller church, they would likely be unpaid staff positions.

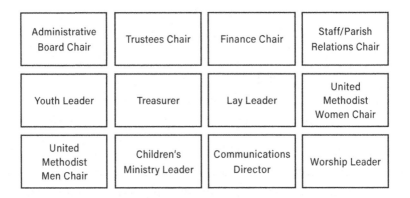

On your chart, write in the names of each person who is currently filling the key leadership positions in your church. If you have someone filling more than one position right now, you may want to list them twice knowing that their replacement may not be able to fill all of those roles.

Once you have your chart complete, then you can work through each person/role and talk about who would be an appropriate back-up for that role. For example, if Shea is your current children's ministry team leader, who in your church do you see as her replacement? It may be someone who is already on that team, it may be someone who is currently listed somewhere else on your chart, or it may be someone else in your church. As you start working through this process with each person/role you will see how there may be potential domino effects of leaders backing up leaders and also discover where you have potential gaps in leadership. This is all great information to have ahead of time, and not discovered the hard way when it is forced upon you.

The leadership replenishment system in your church should serve two different but connected purposes. The first purpose is what we have been focusing on for most of this chapter. A succession planning process for you to see the potential back-ups for each key leadership position. Picture this succession planning as a "top-down" approach to your leadership replenishment. The second purpose is to see who you have in your leadership pipeline and to determine what they need in order to be prepared for potential opportunities. Picture this aspect as the "bottom-up" approach to your leadership replenishment. There should obviously be a lot of overlap to these two purposes.

The term *pipeline* might be new to you. Allow us to explain. Behind each of your current key leaders should be other leaders at various stages of readiness to step into that role or position. For example, a potential back-up for the position of trustees' chairperson who is fully trained and ready now to assume that position could be seen as standing directly behind the person currently in that role. A potential back-up for the position of trustees' chairperson who will need some leader's development training, at least a few years serving on that team, and some mentoring by the current trustees' chairperson could be seen as standing several yards behind the person currently in that role. As you place potential key leadership back-ups behind the people currently filling those roles based on their readiness, you are creating a pipeline. This pipeline concept can be seen as back-ups for either specific positions and roles within the church, or just as a more general back-up for key leadership roles overall. Both concepts have value.

> We hope this conversation on leadership replenishment has gotten you thinking about the appointment process in your conference.

Bishops, district superintendents, and other members of cabinet: We hope this conversation on leadership replenishment has gotten you thinking about the appointment process in your conference. Go back and reread this chapter from the perspective of your experiences with filling pastor openings in your district or in the overall conference. Every year we have pastors who retire, leave the ministry, ask to be moved to another church, or get called to their heavenly home. In some cases, those openings are sudden and unexpected, and in other cases we know them many months or even years before they happen. Would you categorize your appointment process overall as more reactive or more proactive? How are you currently preparing pastors for their next church, especially when that next church is larger than where they are currently serving? What would one step in the proactive direction look like for your appointment process?

Before you move to the next chapter, take a few minutes now to answer the following questions:

What has been a key learning for you from this chapter on leadership replenishment systems? What experience have you had in the past with succession planning?

Where is your church today in this process of identifying and preparing back-ups for each of the key leadership positions in your ministry? What ONE step are you committed to taking this year?

Who in your church, community, district, conference, or else-where will you partner with to grow in your understanding and application of the concept of leadership replenishment systems?

Prayer

Lord, we come to you asking for vision to see beyond ourselves. Give us the ability to see the ways you have gifted each leader in our ministry. Allow us to see the potential you see in us and in others. May we be true to the ways you have blessed each leader and grow them into your image. Amen.

CHAPTER NINE

Fruitful Harvest

Jesus told this parable: "A man owned a fig tree planted in his vineyard. He came looking for fruit on it and found none. He said to his gardener, 'Look, I've come looking for fruit on this fig tree for the past three years, and I've never found any. Cut it down! Why should it continue depleting the soil's nutrients?' The gardener responded, 'Lord, give it one more year, and I will dig around it and give it fertilizer. Maybe it will produce fruit next year; if not, then you can cut it down.'"

Luke 13:6-17

Don't mistake activity for achievement.

John Wooden

God wants your ministry to be fruitful. When you look at all of the different ecosystems around the world, you see how the God of them all has equipped them to produce fruit for his kingdom. We believe that you, too, want your ministry to bear fruit. No matter the size, location, worship style, or many other factors of your church, it can and should be fruitful.

The leaders in your church, you included, are the ecologists who tend to the ecosystem of your ministry to be sure it is as fruitful as possible. While the ecologist monitors the health of the ecosystem, the conservationist takes steps to actively help the ecosystem grow. As you develop leaders in your church, they become your conservationists by actively engaging the ecosystem by planting new seeds in the appropriate seasons, pruning when necessary, and knowing when it is time to cut down, and when it is better to fertilize and give more time. This is never an exact science. No church leader ever gets it right every time. Even in the parable of the sower, Jesus told us that only one out of four of the seeds fell on good soil.

> The leaders in your church, you included, are the ecologists who tend to the ecosystem of your ministry to be sure it is as fruitful as possible.

One key to being fruitful in your ministry is to be clear on what fruit looks like. In other words, what difference are you trying to make with the leadership pathway you are creating for your church? The best place to start is back in chapter two where we talked about prayer. Through prayer and discernment, identify what God wants to see as fruit for your leadership development. We encourage you to do this with others so there will be less chance of only hearing your voice and your own wants and desires.

Once you are clear on where you are going in the long term and what fruit God wants to produce through this process of leadership development, then you will need to set some clear goals to move your ministry in that direction. One or two goals a year would be very appropriate in most churches. Think in terms of small steps. The following tool from the book, *Time Management for the Christian Leader* may help you set more effective goals:

- **Specific** – A specific goal is much more likely to be accomplished than a general goal. The is the "why" element of the goal. Being clear on the "why" is the most important element of any goal.

- **Measurable**– Goals need to be quantifiable. This will help you stay on track, reach target dates, and ultimately achieve the goal. The measurement is NOT the goal, but if the goal does not have a clear "why" then the measurement will often become the goal.

- **Actionable** – The goal should drive people to actually do something or change a behavior. Use strong action verbs and avoid words that might allow the goal to be accomplished without any real changes.

- **Results-Oriented** – The achievement of the goal should move you closer to God's vision and your long-term fruitfulness in ministry. Not just more work.

- **Time-Based** – There should be a clear completion date. This will allow you to break the goal down into smaller steps with milestone dates. The goal should create a sense of urgency.

- **Eternal** – Completion of the goal should have the potential for Kingdom advancement. There should be room for God to work, and in the end, God should get all the glory.

- **Recorded** – Writing the goal down ensures you and everyone else are clear on the goal and it will help communicate it to everyone else. Clarity on the goal is the first step toward completion. [7]

---

7 Willard, Ken. *Time Management for the Christian Leader.* Abingdon Press. 2015.

A dream written down with a date becomes a goal. A goal broken down into steps becomes a plan. A plan backed by action becomes a reality.

Greg Reid

Setting effective goals is of course only the beginning. In the book, *The 4 Disciplines of Execution*[8], the authors talk about "The Whirlwind." These are things that are so urgent they require our attention right now and those things that are just part of our day-to-day, week-to-week, month-to-month, year-to-year activities. Sound familiar? We bet you could make a list of those items right now. Those whirlwind activities can take up the majority of our time each day. We do not have the option of just ignoring them or in many cases handing them off to other people. Our challenge as leaders is being disciplined enough with the non-whirlwind time we have to use it focused on our goals. Our suggestion to you is to work together as leaders to set a few strong goals for this overall process of leadership development and then establish milestone check-in dates along the way to each goal. For example, if you plan to be 100 percent completed with a certain goal in one year, it might be logical to expect you to complete 25 percent of the goal every three months. This is not intended to be an exact science, just to give you targets to shoot at along the way to completing the goal. The most important part of this type of check-in process is maintaining the calendar along the way. This will help to keep the goal and the process in front of you. This should provide

---

8 McChesney, Chris, Sean Covey, and Jim Huling. *The 4 Disciplines of Execution: Achieving Your Wildly Important Goals.* Free Press. 2012.

some accountability in the form of the other leaders on your team putting the dates on their calendars and you holding each other accountable.

We would like to share one more concept with you concerning leadership development: a process for evaluating your work. In 1954, Donald Kirkpatrick created the 'four level' model for evaluating training courses. This had a major impact in the training world and continues to be used today by all types of organizations all over the world. As a leader, we are sure you have at least seen some form of these evaluations. Here is a brief explanation of the four levels:

- **Level One** focuses on what those who participated in the training thought about the experience. Are they satisfied? In the training world this is known as a "smile sheet." Are they smiling? Think about the last time you attended a workshop or took a class of some type and they gave you a one-page evaluation at the end. That is a level one evaluation. Important, but does not really tell us much about the effectiveness of the training. A person might love the training, give five stars for everything, and still go back and do nothing different. We could do a workshop on how to make coffee. You could attend the workshop, think we are great trainers, give us five stars on all areas, but never make any coffee.

- **Level Two** builds on level one evaluations and then concentrates of validating the retention of knowledge or skills, and in some cases a change in an area of attitude. In order to validate this type of learning, there is usually a test of some form used either at the end of the training or shortly thereafter. The most common example all of us have experienced is in a school classroom. The teacher or instructor shares information, we often will do some reading, maybe some group work, and then there is a test to score our retention of the knowledge. Again, this can be very helpful but does not always indicate that the students or participants will actually use the new knowledge. Back to the coffee training workshop, you might love the session, and pass a test on how to make coffee, but still never actually make coffee.

- **Level Three** builds on the first two and focused on the actual transfer of knowledge to application. This level of evaluation is designed to validate a behavior change in the participants of the training. In most cases, this is done through direct observation and will usually take place several months after the training session. Using the coffee making workshop again, this would require one of us or another agent to see you making coffee the way we taught you in the training.

- **Level Four** builds on the other three and focuses on results. While the results can be anything those in charge want them to be, for this to be used correctly, the desired results must be identified prior to the training taking place. For example, a restaurant may want to improve its customer service scores. It has all employees complete a customer service training course. The organization typically identifies where they are now "X" and where they want to be "Y" and then creates a training course of some type to move them to that goal. This level of evaluation is how they would measure those results. Just having people take the training is not a good result to measure, especially if that attendance or participation is mandatory or could be seen as such by the participants. Using our coffee training example, we might be trying to lower the monthly cost of coffee supplies and we would be able to see if those results were being reflected on the monthly expense reports.

Here is an example of a standard level one evaluation. A five-point rating scale of:

(1) Poor/Low

(2) Fair

(3) Good/Medium

(4) Strong

(5) Excellent/High is often used on these evaluations

1. The objectives were clearly stated for the training and met.

2. The materials were useful and relevant.

3. The topics covered were what I expected.

4. The knowledge of the trainer added richness to my learning experience.

5. The pace of the session was appropriate.

6. The environment was free of distractions so I could focus on the course.

7. I was fully engaged during the session.

8. I learned things in this session that are relevant to me and my ministry.

9. I intend to use what I learned in this session in my ministry.

10. I would rate the session overall as a: _____.

Then three open-ended questions:

- What, if anything, would you suggest to improve this course in the future?

- What is your biggest take-away from this session?

- What other comments do you have?

Properly evaluating all elements of your leadership pathway can help you see where you are producing fruit and where you may need to make some adjustments. Start with the level one types of evaluations and then build up a level as you continue to expand and grow your process. Most churches have a person who has the gifts to track these evaluations and provide you with the information you need along the way.

> Properly evaluating all elements of your leadership pathway can help you see where you are producing fruit and where you may need to make some adjustments.

Even after the awakening due to the fire, the Cuyahoga River took decades to become a flourishing watershed and for the ecosystem to recover. Creating and implementing a process of leadership development will also take time. Don't give up, stick to the established goals, stick to the intended outcomes, and remember the difference God is calling you to make.

As we come to the end of the book, take a look back through each chapter. We hope you took some time at the end of each chapter to answer the questions and maybe make some notes. Review all of those notes and your responses to the questions now.

In the spaces below, record a key learning or two from each chapter:

1. The Church as an Ecosystem

2. Prayer, Scripture, and Preparation

3. Study the System

4. Leadership Development Approaches

5. Creating Your Leadership Development Pathway

6. Covenants, Coaching, and Culture

7. Small Church Leadership

8. Leadership Pipeline

9. Fruitful Harvest

Take a few minutes now to answer the following questions:

- Who will you partner with on this journey?

- When will you invite them to join you?

- How will you ensure there is accountability in place for your plans and goals?

- What will you do next? When will you do it?

Prayer

Lord, may our efforts and plans follow the leading of your Spirit and not our own wants and desires. You are Lord of the Harvest. May we produce good fruit for your kingdom. Be with us on this journey as we grow and develop leaders. Work through us, use us as servants, we desire to be lights who point others to you. In the wonderful and risen name of your son, Jesus, Amen.

Appendix 1

Common Church Leadership Positions

(not a complete listing)

- Ordained, certified, professional clergy

- Part-time or full-time local pastors

- Lay leaders

- United Methodist Women president

- United Methodist Men president

- Certified Lay Servant

- Certified Lay Speaker

- Certified Lay Minister

- Trustee Chairperson

- Finance Chairperson

- Staff/Parish (or Pastor/Parish) Relations Chairperson

- Sunday School Teacher

- Small Group Leader

- Hospitality Team Leader

- Director of Christian Education

- Youth Leader

- Worship or Music Director

- Children's Ministry Director

- Connections Director

- Administrative Board Chairperson

- Communications Director

- Missions Team Leader

- Outreach Team Leader

- Executive Pastor

- Diaconal Minister

- Deacon

- Ministry Coordinator

- Nominations Committee Chairperson

- Youth Pastor

- Retired Pastor

- Any Member of Church Staff

- Yes, that position which is not on this list--they are a leader if they are in a position to influence others.

Appendix 2
Leadership Reading List

(grouped by course topics)

Accountability

Principle-Centered Leadership
   by Stephen R. Covey

*Winning with Accountability: The Secret Language of
   High-Performing Organizations*
   by Henry J. Evans

*Winning on Purpose: How to Organize Congregations to
   Succeed in Their Mission*
   by John Edmund Kaiser

Catalytic Capacity

The New Adapters: Shaping Ideas to Fit Your Congregation
   by Jacob Armstrong

Just Say Yes! Unleashing People for Ministry
   by Robert Schnase

*The Power of R.E.A.L. Changing Lives. Changing Churches
   Changing Communities*
   by Joe Daniels Jr.

Change Leadership

Managing Transitions: Making the Most of Change
   by William Bridges

Switch: How to Change Things When Change is Hard
by Chip Heath and Dan Heath

Connecting for Change
by Joe Daniels Jr. and Christie Latona

Good Idea. Now What?: How to Move Ideas to Execution
by Charles T. Lee

New Wine, New Wineskins: How African American Congregations Can Reach New Generations
by Douglas Powe, Jr.

Leading Change
by John P. Kotter

The Power of Habit: Why We Do What We Do in Life and Business
by Charles Duhigg

Leading Congregational Change: A Practical Guide for the Transformational Journey
by Jim Herrington, Mike Bonem, and James H. Furr

Who Moved My Cheese?
by Spencer Johnson

Our Iceberg Is Melting: Changing and Succeeding Under Any Conditions
by John P. Kotter

Managing Polarities in Congregations: Eight Keys for Thriving Faith Communities
by Roy M. Oswald and Barry Johnson

Church Health

The Emotionally Healthy Church
   by Peter Scazzero

The Healthy Small Church: Treatment for the Big Issues
   by Dennis Bickers

Shift 2.0: Helping congregations back into the game of effective ministry
   by Phil Maynard

Renovate or Die: Ten Ways to Focus Your Church on Mission
   by Kay Kotan and Bob Farr

The Unstuck Church: Equipping Churches to Experience Sustained Health
   by Tony Morgan

Mission Possible: A Simple Structure for Missional Effectiveness
   by Blake Bradford and Kay Kotan

Ten Prescriptions for a Healthy Church
   by Kay Kotan and Bob Farr

Small Church Checkup: Assessing Your Church's Health and Creating a Treatment Plan
   by Kay Kotan and Phil Schroeder

Gear Up! Nine Essential Process for the Optimized Church
   by Kay Kotan

Conflict Resolution/Transformation

The Anatomy of Peace: Resolving the Heart of Conflict
   by The Arbinger Institute

Crucial Confrontations: Tools for Resolving Broken Promises, Violated Expectations, and Bad Behavior
by Kerry Patterson, Joseph Grenny, Ron McMillan, and Al Switzler

Crucial Conversations: Tools for Talking When Stakes Are High
by Kerry Patterson, Joseph Grenny, Ron McMillan, and Al Switzler

The Peacemaking Pastor: A Biblical Guide to Resolving Church Conflict
by Alfred Poirier

Leadership and Self-Deception: Getting Out of The Box
by The Arbinger Institute

Discipleship

Simple Church: Returning to God's Process for Making Disciples
by Thom S. Rainer and Eric Geiger

Stride: Creating a Discipleship Pathway for Your Church
by Mike Schreiner and Ken Willard

Membership to Discipleship Growing Mature Disciples Who Make Disciples
by Phil Maynard

Evangelism

Unbinding the Gospel: Real Life Evangelism
by Martha Grace Reese

Transforming Evangelism: The Wesleyan Way of Sharing Faith
F. Douglas Powe Jr.

Get Their Name: Grow Your Church by Building
  New Relationships
  by Bob Farr, Doug Anderson, and Kay Kotan

Faith in the Calling of God

The Call: Finding and Fulfilling the Central Purpose of Your Life
  by Os Guinness

S.H.A.P.E. Finding and Fulfilling Your Unique Purpose for Life
  by Erik Rees

Growing New Leaders

Growing Young: Six Essential Strategies to Help Young
  People Discover and Love Your Church
  by Kara Powell, Jake Mulder, and Brad Griffin

Chess, Not Checkers: Elevate Your Leadership Game
  by Mark Miller

Leaders Made Here: Building a Leadership Culture
  by Mark Miller

Not Safe For Church: Ten Commandments for Reaching New
  Generations
  by Douglas Powe Jr. and Jasmine Rose Smothers

Blank Slate: Write Your Own Rules for a 22nd Century
  Church Movement
  by Lia McIntosh, Jasmine Rose Smothers, Rodney Thomas Smothers

Justice and Advocacy

Toxic Charity: How Churches and Charities Hurt Those They Help
by Robert T. Lupton

Pastors

Unleashing the Word
by Adam Hamilton

Communicating for a Change: Seven Keys to Irresistible Communication
by Andy Stanley and Lane Jones

Speaking Well: Essential Skills for Speakers, Leaders, and Preachers
by Adam Hamilton

The Necessary Nine: Things Effective Pastors Do Differently
by Kay Kotan and Bob Farr

Perseverance

Failing Forward: Turning Mistakes Into Stepping Stones
by John C. Maxwell

Spiritual Formation

Celebration of Discipline: The Path to Spiritual Growth
by Richard J. Foster

Soul Feast: An Invitation to the Christian Spiritual Life
by Marjorie J. Thompson

Sacred Rhythms: Arranging Our Lives for Spiritual Transformation
by Ruth Haley Barton

Strategic Planning

Advanced Strategic Planning: A New Model for Church and Ministry Leaders
by Aubrey Malphurs

Visioneering: God's Blueprint for Developing and Maintaining Personal Vision
by Andy Stanley

Church Growth Flywheel: 5 Practical Systems to Drive Growth at Your Church
by Rich Birch

Doing the Math of Mission: Fruits, Faithfulness and Metrics
by Gil Rendle

Raising the Roof: The Pastoral-To-Program Size Transition
by Alice Mann

Bearing Fruit: Ministry with Real Results
by Lovett H. Weems, Jr. and Tom Berlin

Stewardship

Not Your Parents' Offering Plate: A New Vision for Financial Stewardship
by J. Clif Christopher

Additional Key Leadership Books

Beyond the First Visit: The Complete Guide to Connecting Guests to Your Church
by Gary L. McIntosh

Canoeing the Mountains: Christian Leadership in Uncharted Territory
by Tod Bolsinger

Direct Hit: Aiming Real Leaders at the Mission Field
by Paul D. Borden

Five Practices of Fruitful Congregations
by Robert Schnase

Fusion: Turning First-Time Guests into Fully-Engaged Members of Your Church
by Nelson Searcy

Get Out of That Box! Realizing Personal Potential and Enhancing Team Collaboration to Move Ministry Forward
by Anne Bosarge

Good to Great: Why Some Companies Make the Leap . . . and Others Don't
by Jim Collins

Impact! Reclaiming the Call of Lay Ministry
by Kay Kotan and Blake Bradford

Lead Like Jesus: Lessons from the Greatest Leadership Role Model of All Time
by Ken Blanchard and Phil Hodges

Leadership 101: What Every Leader Needs to Know
by John C. Maxwell

Ministry Nuts and Bolts: What They Don't Teach Pastors in Seminary
by Aubrey Malphurs

Move: What 1,000 Churches Reveal About Spiritual Growth
by Greg L. Hawkins and Cally Parkinson

Raising the Roof: The Pastoral to Program Size Transition
by Alice Mann

Seven Practices of Effective Ministry
by Andy Stanley, Lane Jones, and Reggie Joiner

Start This Stop That: Do the Things That Grow Your Church
by Jim Cowart and Jennifer Cowart

The Four Disciplines of Execution: Achieving Your Wildly Important Goals
by Sean Covey, Chris McChesney, and Jim Hulling

The Advantage: Why Organizational Health Trumps Everything Else in Business
by Patrick Lencioni

The Emotionally Healthy Leader: How Transforming Your Inner Life Will Deeply Transform Your Church, Team, and the World
by Peter Scazzero

The Five Dysfunctions of a Team: A Leadership Fable
by Patrick Lencioni

Time Management for the Christian Leader: Or How to Squeeze Blood from a Turnip
by Ken Willard

Ultimately Responsible: When You're in Charge of Igniting a Ministry
by Sue Nilson Kibbey

Beyond the Bible: Must Read Books for Leaders

(all are listed above, too)

Good to Great

Canoeing the Mountains

Managing Transitions

Leadership and the One-Minute Manager

The Five Dysfunctions of a Team

Now, Discover Your Strengths

The Four Disciplines of Execution

Appendix 3

Leadership Covenant Example

The following is an example of a leadership covenant a church or a learning community might use. We encourage you to adapt this covenant to fit your needs. As stated before, we recommend that any group of leaders develops their covenant together as a group and where possible are not just asked to sign something they did not play a part in creating.

As a leader of _____ Church I will:

Protect the unity of our church:

- By praying for our church, pastors, staff, and leaders daily (1 Thessalonians 1:1-2)

- By supporting and communicating the mission, vision, and values [insert mission and vision statements]

- By following the leadership of the church (Hebrews 13:17)

- By acting in love toward others, using positive and encouraging words (Ephesians 4:12)

- By refusing to gossip (Ephesians 4:29).

Serve the ministry of our church:

- By having a servant's heart (Philippians 2:3-4,7)

- By having a dedication to excellence in all things (Colossians 3:23-24)

- By using my gifts and abilities where called (1 Peter 4:10)

- By being accountable to others in my ministry area (Hebrews 13:17).

Support the spiritual growth of myself, others, and our church:

- By taking the next steps on my path of discipleship (2 Peter 1:2-8)

- By encouraging those around to become fully devoted followers of Christ (1 Thessalonians 5:11)

- By inviting the unchurched to attend worship services and events (Luke 14:23)

- By modeling radical hospitality to all (Romans 15:7).

- Continue to grow as a Christian leader (Matthew 20:26)

- By taking my responsibility seriously and leading my ministry to the best of my ability (Colossians 3:23)

- By participating in leadership training and development opportunities (1 Timothy 4:14)

- By seeking out opportunities to learn and grow (Proverbs 1:5).

Signed: _____ Date: _____

About the Authors

Kelly Brown

Kelly and his family live in Canton, Ohio. He is the Director of Congregational Vitality for the East Ohio Conference of the United Methodist Church.

Kelly is an Ordained Elder in the United Methodist Church and an Associate Certified Coach with the International Coaching Federation. He has over twenty years of ministry experience in different settings, including eight years in his current position teaching, coaching, and consulting with churches and leaders.

Ken Willard

Ken and his wife Mary live in Winfield, West Virginia. He is the Director of Discipleship, Leadership, and Congregational Vitality for the West Virginia Annual Conference of the United Methodist Church.

Ken is a Professionally Certified Coach with the International Coach Federation and works with Coaching4Clergy as part of their faculty. He has been teaching and coaching leaders for over twenty years with both businesses and churches.

As an author, Ken has published several other books including:

- *Time Management for the Christian Leader: Or How to Squeeze Blood from a Turnip*
- *Stride: Creating a Discipleship Pathway for Your Church*
- *Stride Participant Workbook: Creating a Discipleship Pathway for Your Life*

Other Books

from Market Square

marketsquarebooks.com

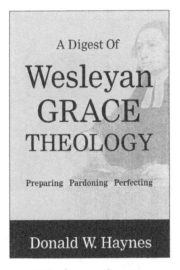

Wesleyan Grace Theology

Dr. Donald Haynes

Where Do We Go From Here?

24 United Methodist Writers

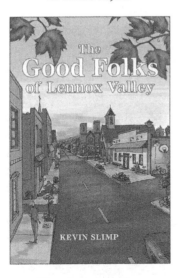

The Good Folks of Lennox Valley

Kevin Slimp

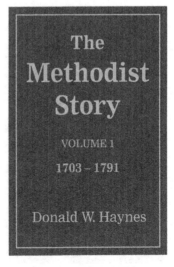

The Methodist Story Volume I • 1703-1791

Dr. Donald Haynes

Grow Your Faith

with these books from Market Square

marketsquarebooks.com

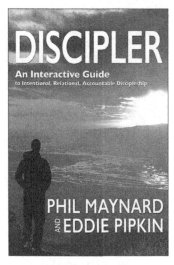

Discipler

Phil Maynard & Eddie Pipkin

Hear It, See It, Risk It

Steve Cordle

A Christian Teenager's
Guide to Surviving High School

Ashley Conner

Understanding Your Call
**11 Biblical Figures Understand
Their Calls from God**

by 10 United Methodist Leaders

Grow Your Faith

with these books from Market Square

marketsquarebooks.com

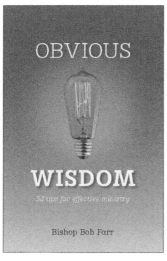

Obvious Wisdom

Bishop Bob Farr

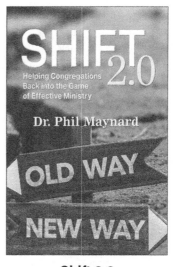

Shift 2.0

Phil Maynard

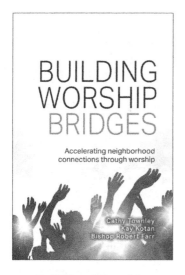

Building Worship Bridges

Cathy Townley

Get Out of That Box!

Anne Bosarge

Latest Titles
from Market Square Books
marketsquarebooks.com

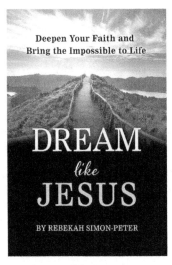

Dream Like Jesus
Bring the Impossible to Life
Rebekah Simon-Peter

From Franchise
To Local Dive
Available November 2019

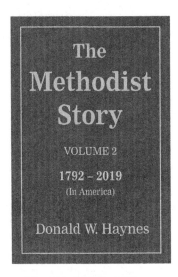

The Methodist Story
Volume 2 ▪ 1792-2019
Dr. Donald W. Haynes

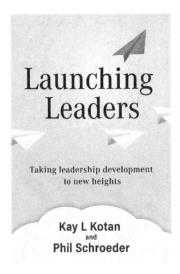

Launching Leaders
Leadership Development
Kay Kotan and Phil Schroeder

Latest Titles

from Market Square Books

marketsquarebooks.com

From Heaven To Earth

Wil Cantrell & Paul Seay

Tidings of Comfort and Joy

Charles W. Maynard

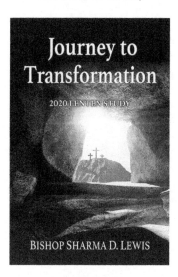

Journey to Transformatio

Bishop Sharma D. Lewis

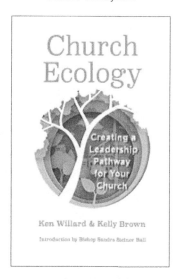

Church Ecology

Ken Willard & Kelly Brown

Made in the USA
Coppell, TX
04 September 2020